Limitation of Actions

by Richard D. James, LL.M., Solicitor, Lecturer in Law at the University of Wales, Cardiff

Tolley Publishing Company Ltd
A UNITED NEWSPAPERS PUBLICATION

ISBN 0 85459 757-3

First published 1993

A catalogue record for this book is available from the British Library

Published by
Tolley Publishing Company Limited
Tolley House
2 Addiscombe Road
Croydon
Surrey
CR9 5AF
081-686 9141

Photoset by
Promenade Graphics Ltd, Gloucester

Printed and bound in Great Britain by
Hobbs the Printers, Southampton

Limitation of Actions

Tolley Publishing Company Limited

Preface

I became interested in the limitation of actions when I was in practice as a solicitor and my aim in writing this book has been to provide a clear and reasonably concise statement of the law suited to the needs of practitioners. I have therefore given closest attention to the matters which are of daily concern to them. In particular there is fairly detailed discussion of procedural issues, including amendment after expiry of the limitation period, dismissal for want of prosecution and renewal of writs.

The law is stated as it stood on 4 May 1993.

Richard James

Contents

Table of Statutes

Table of Statutory Instruments

Table of Cases

Chapter 1

Introduction

1. Policy

There seem to be two policy aspects to the rules of limitation, though they are not entirely distinct from each other. First it is thought to be in the general public interest that at some stage a dispute should be regarded as automatically at an end in the absence of proceedings. The finality provided by the limitation period thus brings an important element of certainty to people's dealings. The second concerns more the position of potential litigants themselves. It is accepted that a defendant should be protected from a stale claim made at a time when the evidence essential to his case may no longer be available. This was identified as the primary purpose of the limitation period by Lord Griffiths in *Donovan* v *Gwentoys* (1990). Conversely the plaintiff is required to make his claim without unreasonable delay so that the action can be tried while the recollection of witnesses is still clear. These in essence were the policies identified by the Law Reform Committee in its Final Report on Limitation of Actions (Cmnd 6923 para 1.7). In *Cartledge* v *E Jopling & Sons* (1963) Lord Pearce described the Limitation Act 1939, the main statute then in force, as "a practical compromise intended to encourage and secure reasonable diligence in litigation and to protect defendants from stale claims when the evidence which might have answered them has perished".

2. Historical background

There are no limitation periods at common law. Equity developed the doctrine of laches at an early stage but otherwise the policies just mentioned have been implemented exclusively by statute. The Limitation Act 1623 created a limitation period of six years for common law actions and it was followed by various other Acts. The most important were the Civil Procedure Act 1833, the Real Property Limitation Acts 1833 and 1874 and the Public Authorities Protection Act 1893. They were all superseded by the Limitation Act 1939. This remained in force until 1981 but important changes were made in the meanwhile by several other statutes, notably the Law Reform (Limitation of Actions) Act 1954 and the Limitation Acts 1963 and 1975. The law was again consolidated by the Limitation Act 1980 which is of course still in force. Amendments have been made to it by the Administration of Justice Act 1985, the Latent Damage Act 1986 and the Consumer Protection Act 1987.

The general trend of recent reform has been towards individual justice at the expense of certainty. In personal injury claims and negligence actions generally limitation periods have been introduced which run from the date when the plaintiff knew or should have known the crucial facts of his case. The court now has a discretion in both personal injury and defamation cases to allow actions to be brought outside the normal limitation period. In negligence cases (other than personal injury claims) and actions under the Consumer Protection Act 1987 (including personal injury claims) a degree of certainty has been preserved by the introduction of rules preventing claims after the expiry of "long-stop" periods.

3. The present statutory framework

The Limitation Act 1980 is reproduced as amended in Appendix 1. The ordinary time limits are contained in Part 1 of the Act. These limits are subject to possible extension or exclusion under the provisions of Part 2. The most important of these are those relating to disability (s 28), fraud, concealment and mistake (s 32) and the court's discretion mentioned above to disapply the normal time limits in personal injury actions (s 33). Part 3 contains various supplementary provisions. The following are the most important of the limitation periods laid down in Part 1.

Action	*Limitation period*
(*i*) An action for damages for personal injuries (other than under the Consumer Protection Act 1987).	Three years from the date when certain crucial facts were reasonably discoverable by the plaintiff, subject to extension at the discretion of the court (s 11, s 33).
(*ii*) An action for damages for personal injuries under the Consumer Protection Act 1987.	As above, though subject to a ten year "long-stop" period running from the time when the defective goods were put into circulation (s 11A, s 33).
(*iii*) A negligence action (other than a personal injury claim) where the damage is not reasonably discoverable when it occurs.	The more favourable of either three years from the date of discoverability or six years from the date of accrual of the cause of action, subject to a maximum of fifteen years from the defendant's last negligent act or omission (s 14A, s 14B).
(*iv*) Any other negligence action.	Six years from the accrual of the cause of action subject to a maximum of fifteen years from the defendant's last negligent act or omission (s 2, s 14B).

(*v*) A defamation action.	Three years from accrual of the cause of action subject to a judicial discretion to extend (s 4A, s 32A).
(*vi*) Any other tort action (except conversion).	Six years from accrual of the cause of action (s 2).
(*vii*) A contract action (unless the contract is under seal).	Six years from accrual of the cause of action (s 5).
(*viii*) An action to enforce an award (unless the submission is by an instrument under seal).	Six years from accrual of the cause of action (s 7).
(*ix*) An action on a specialty.	Twelve years from accrual of the cause of action (s 8).
(*x*) An action for a sum recoverable by virtue of a statute (other than the Civil Liability (Contribution) Act 1978).	Six years from accrual of the cause of action (s 9).
(*xi*) An action for contribution under the Civil Liability (Contribution) Act 1978.	Two years from the date of the judgment or settlement (s 10).
(*xii*) An action to recover land.	Twelve years from accrual of the right of action (s 15).
(*xiii*) An action for breach of trust.	Normally six years from accrual of the right of action (s 21(3)).
(*xiv*) An action claiming any interest in the personal estate of a deceased person.	Twelve years from accrual of the right to receive the property (s 22).

Chapter 2

Cases outside the Limitation Act 1980

Part 1 of the Limitation Act 1980 gives the ordinary time limits for actions of most types (s 1(1)). By s 38(1) "action" includes any proceedings in a court of law including an ecclesiastical court. The enforcement of a judgment is not within the meaning of the word and the relevant time limits are those contained in rules of court (*Lamb & Sons* v *Rider* (1948), *National Westminster Bank plc* v *Powney & others* (1989)). Because there are no limitation periods at common law an action will have no time limit at all if it is not covered by the Act or other legislation. This is so in the case of a probate action (*Re Flynn deceased* (1982)) and in the case of proceedings against a solicitor under the inherent supervisory jurisdiction of the court (*Bray* v *Stuart West & Co* (1989)). Section 34 makes the Act and any other limitation enactment applicable to arbitrations in the same way as to actions.

By s 36 certain of the Act's time limits do not apply, except in a limited way, to claims for equitable relief. Section 37 governs the application of the Act to the Crown. Section 39 provides that the Act does not apply at all where a period of limitation is prescribed by or under any other enactment. Section 40(1) and Sch 2 contain transitional provisions and the Foreign Limitation Periods Act 1984 makes foreign limitation periods applicable in certain circumstances to the exclusion of those of English law.

1. Equity

Courts of equity developed the doctrines of laches and acquiescence. They were not bound by the statutes of limitation unless their wording expressly included proceedings for equitable relief, though the practice evolved of applying statutory time limits by analogy where appropriate. This was mainly in cases where the equitable remedy was similar to the legal remedy or was in aid of legal rights (*Knox* v *Gye* (1872)). The Limitation Act 1980 applies whatever the nature of the claim but this is subject to s 36. Subsection (1) provides that s 2 (tort), s 4A (defamation), s 5 (contract), s 7 (awards), s 8 (specialties), s 9 (sums recoverable by statute) and s 24 (actions to enforce judgments) do not apply to claims for specific performance, injunctions or other equitable relief, except by analogy in the same way as corresponding statutory time limits were applied before the Limitation Act 1939. By s 36(2) the equitable jurisdiction to refuse relief on the ground of acquiescence or laches is unaffected by the Act.

There is an overlap in the ground covered by these two doctrines. Acquiescence is the equitable defence available in certain circumstances against a plaintiff who has shown indifference to the infringement of his rights (*Crabb* v *Arun DC* (1976)). It will not apply unless he was aware of the relevant facts or at least could have discovered them with reasonable diligence. Where the plaintiff is not aware of the infringement at the time but discovers it later, there may be acquiescence if his subsequent conduct is such that to grant him relief would be an injustice to the defendant. Injustice to blameless third parties will also be taken into account. Delay is not a necessary part of the doctrine; the plaintiff's conduct at the very time of the infringement of his rights may suffice. Where the plaintiff's conduct takes the form of inexcusable delay at a time when he knew or should have known of his rights, he may be denied relief through the doctrine of laches. The court considers all the circumstances, including the conduct of both parties. It remains a requirement that injustice would result to the defendant if relief were granted (*Re Bailey Hay & Co Ltd* (1971), *Gapp* v *Chamberlain* (1991)).

There is no room for the operation of acquiescence or laches in an action for which a statutory limitation period is applicable either expressly or by analogy (*Archbold* v *Scully* (1861), *Younghusband* v *Coutts & Co* (1962)). The position can therefore be summarised as follows. Limitation periods not mentioned in s 36(1) apply even where equitable relief is sought and nothing else is relevant. Where s 36(1) does apply (or where the claim is not covered by the Act at all) a statutory period will in some cases be applied by analogy. Otherwise a claim for equitable relief is subject only to the doctrines of acquiescence and laches.

Claims for injunctions in contract and tort actions are no doubt the most important category of cases left to the rules of equity by s 36(1). It is necessary to distinguish between interlocutory and final injunctions. It is settled that delay short of the statutory period applicable to the plaintiff's legal rights does not affect the availability of a final injunction (*Pride of Derby Assoc.* v *British Celanese* (1953)). But an application for an interlocutory injunction may be seriously prejudiced by delay on the part of the plaintiff, all the more so if the defendant has incurred expenses or otherwise changed his position in the meanwhile (*G.W.R.* v *Oxford Railway* (1853)).

2. The Crown

The Limitation Act 1980 s 37(1) states that except as provided otherwise elsewhere in the Act it applies to proceedings by or against the Crown in the same way as it applies to proceedings between subjects. For this purpose proceedings by or against the Crown include proceedings by or against the Duke of Cornwall or Her Majesty in right of the Duchy of Lancaster and also proceedings involving a government department, an officer of the Crown or any person acting on behalf of the Crown (s 37(3)). Certain exceptions to this rule are contained in s 37(2). They are proceedings by the Crown for the recovery of any tax or duty or interest thereon, forfeiture proceedings under the Customs and Excise Acts and proceedings in respect of the forfeiture of a ship. The wording of the subsection suggests that the last of these exceptions applies generally and not merely where the Crown is a party. In addition s 37(6) removes from the ambit of the Act the prerogative right of the Crown or the Duke of Cornwall to any gold or silver mine. Section 37(1) is stated to be without prejudice to s 39; see below. The result is that even where the Crown is a party, the Limitation Act does not apply to any action for which a limitation period is prescribed by another enactment. Finally Schedule 1 Part II of the Act contains modifications to s 15 (actions to recover land) which apply where the Crown is involved.

The Foreign Limitation Periods Act 1984 (see page 9) is binding on the Crown (1984 Act s 6). The Latent Damage Act 1986 s 1 and s 2 (see Chapter 6) operate by adding new sections to the Limitation Act itself. Section 3 is binding on the Crown but as regards tort liability no further than the Crown is made liable by the Crown Proceedings Act 1947 (1986 Act s 3(7)).

3. Other statutes

By s 39 the Limitation Act 1980 does not apply to any action or arbitration for which a period of limitation is prescribed by or under any other enactment whenever passed. The whole of the Act is inapplicable in such cases including the provisions in Part II relating to the extension or exclusion of the time limits of Part I. Any relevant provision of this sort will therefore be found, if at all, only in the individual statute in question. Statutes containing limitation rules of their own are numerous. The most important are mentioned below with brief accounts of the main provisions of those most likely to be of concern in civil litigation.

(a) Employment and discrimination

Applications to tribunals under the legislation in this area have to be made within comparatively short time limits, normally three months. The starting date for the period depends on the nature of the right in question. The main statutes are the Sex Discrimination Act 1975, the Race Relations Act 1976 and the Employment Protection (Consolidation) Act 1978.

(b) Transport

Various conventions relating to the international transport of passengers or property have been given the force of law by the statutes mentioned below. Their limitation periods are typically shorter than those which would otherwise apply in England and Wales.

(i) The Carriage of Goods by Sea Act 1971

This gives effect to the Hague Visby Rules, which apply to the international carriage of goods by sea and require proceedings to be commenced within one year of delivery of the goods or, in a case of non-delivery, the date when they should have been delivered.

(ii) The Merchant Shipping Act 1979

This concerns accidents to passengers on international crossings and loss of or damage to their luggage. The normal limitation period is two years from the date of disembarkation or the date when disembarkation should have occurred in the case of a fatal accident during the journey. Where a passenger's injuries lead to his death after disembarkation, the two year period runs from the date of the death, though this is subject to a maximum of three years from the date of disembarkation.

(iii) The Carriage by Air Act 1961

This applies to international flights and creates a time limit of two years for actions for personal injuries to passengers (including fatal accident claims) or for loss of or damage to baggage or cargo. It runs from the date of arrival of the aircraft at its destination or the date when it should have arrived or on which the carriage stopped.

(iv) Carriage of Goods by Road Act 1965

By this Act actions arising out of the international transport of goods by road are subject to a time limit of one year, or three years where there has been wilful misconduct. The period runs from the date of delivery in the case of partial loss or damage or delay. For total loss it runs from the thirtieth day after the agreed delivery date or, if no such date was agreed, from the sixtieth day after the goods were taken over by the carrier. In other cases it begins three months after the making of the contract of carriage.

(v) Carriage of Passengers by Road Act 1974

When s 1 of this Act comes into force it will give effect to the Convention on the Contract for the International Carriage of Passengers and Luggage by Road, which is set out in the schedule to the Act. The Convention is intended to govern the international carriage of passengers by road. Claims which would fall within the Convention meanwhile continue to be subject to the common law.

Once in force the Act will lay down a limitation period of three years for claims for personal injuries and death running from the date when the person suffering the loss or damage knew or should have known of it, though this is subject to a maximum of five years from the date of the accident. All other actions have a limitation period of one year from the date of the vehicle's arrival at the passenger's destination or, if it failed to arrive, the date when it should have done so.

(vi) International Transport Conventions Act 1983

This deals with the carriage by rail of passengers and property. There is a limitation period of three years for personal injury claims. For fatal accidents the period runs from the date of death, but this is subject to a maximum of five years from the date of the accident. The period for claims in respect of goods is normally one year.

(c) Miscellaneous

(i) The Defective Premises Act 1972

There is in fact nothing in this Act excluding any of the provisions of the Limitation Act 1980 but s 1(5) stipulates the time when a cause of action for breach of the duty created by the Act accrues.

(ii) The Inheritance (Provision for Family and Dependents) Act 1975

An application by a dependent for financial provision must be made within six months of the date of the grant of probate or letters of administration. The court has a discretion to extend this time limit.

(iii) The Magistrates' Courts Act 1980

Section 127 of this Act covers civil as well as criminal matters. The rule is that except as provided otherwise by any other enactment the complaint must be made within six months of the time when the matter of complaint arose.

(iv) The Maritime Conventions Act 1911

This lays down a limitation period of two years for an action in respect of damage or loss to a vessel, her cargo or freight or any property on board or personal injuries (including death) suffered by any person on board caused by the fault of another vessel. Fault is not confined to fault in navigation (*The Norwhale* (1975)). The period runs from the date when the damage, loss or injury was caused and it can be extended by the court at its discretion for as long and on such conditions as it thinks fit. Except in actions against ships of the Crown (which is otherwise bound by the Act) an extension is mandatory if the two year period has been insufficient to give the plaintiff a reasonable opportunity of arresting the defendant vessel within the jurisdiction of the court or within the territorial waters of the country to which the plaintiff's ship belongs or in which the plaintiff resides or has his principal place of business.

(v) The Nuclear Installations Act 1965

By s 15(1) there is a limitation period of thirty years for most actions under the Act. The section also defines the starting point for the period.

(vi) The Post Office Act 1969

An action against the Post Office under s 30 of this Act for loss of or damage to postal packets must be started within twelve months of the date of posting.

4. Foreign limitation periods

The rules of limitation are regarded as procedural and our courts apply their own procedure even when dealing with an action having a foreign element. Before the Foreign Limitation Periods Act 1984 it made no difference if English private international law referred the substantive issues of the case to the law of another jurisdiction. The foreign limitation rules were disregarded, though not if their effect was to extinguish the plaintiff's right rather than merely bar his remedy for then it was a matter of substantive law rather than procedure (*Huber* v *Steiner* (1835)).

The Foreign Limitation Periods Act 1984 reversed the position. It is reproduced in Appendix 3. The basic rule now is that where English private international law refers any matter to the law of another country, any limitation issue relating to that matter is also to be determined by the foreign law (s 1(1)). The possibility that the private international law of the foreign country might refer the issue back to English law is excluded by s 1(5) and s 4(2). However, the time when proceedings are commenced (that is to say the moment when time stops running) is to be decided by English law alone (s 1(3)). Subject to s 4(3), discussed below, the foreign law applies to the exclusion of English law (s 1(1)(a)), except where the substantive issue itself is determined by reference to both a foreign law and English law (s 1(2)). The obvious example is the rule that a defendant is not liable in tort unless his act was tortious both in England and Wales and in the place where it was done (*Boys* v *Chaplin* (1971)). In such a case the limitation rules of both jurisdictions will apply.

In applying the foreign limitation law the English court in general applies any rules of that law relating to the extension, reduction or interruption of the limitation period (s 4(1)). However, these are disregarded in so far as they provide for the extension or interruption of time by reason of the absence of one of the parties from any particular jurisdiction or country (s 2(3)). Where the foreign law confers a discretion on the court, it is to be exercised in the same way as in the foreign jurisdiction so far as practicable (s 1(4)). The court's discretion under English law to refuse equitable relief on the grounds of acquiescence or laches is not affected by the Act but in exercising the discretion the court must have regard to the provisions of the foreign law (s 4(3)).

Section 2(1) creates an imprecise general exception to the basic rule of the Act by excluding s 1 to the extent that its application would conflict with public policy. By s 2(2) there is such a conflict where the application of s 1 would cause undue hardship to an actual or potential party to the action. This subsection was applied in *Jones* v *Trollope Colls Cementation Overseas Ltd* (1990), where the plaintiff's injuries prevented her from issuing proceedings within the short limitation period applicable in Pakistan. Sections 1, 2 and 4 also apply to arbitrations (s 5). Section 3 provides for the recognition of foreign judgments on limitation issues.

5. Transitional provisions

The Limitation Act 1980 came into force on 1 May 1981 (s 41). Its transitional provisions are contained in s 40(1) and Sch 2 para 9. It does not affect any action started before 1 August 1980 or the title to any property which is the subject of any such action. Nor does it enable any action to be brought which was already statute-barred before that date. The Foreign Limitation Periods Act 1984, which came into force on 1 October 1985, contains similar provisions. Section 7(3) provides that the Act does not apply to proceedings commenced before that date or to causes of action already statute-barred at that date under the old law. It does apply where the proceedings are issued after 1 October 1985 even though the cause of action arose before that date (*Jones* v *Trollope Colls Cementation Overseas Ltd*).

Other transitional provisions are discussed in the contexts in which they arise, namely defamation, personal injury claims, the Consumer Protection Act 1987 and the Latent Damage Act 1986.

Chapter 3

The running of time

1. Accrual of the cause of action

Most of the limitation periods laid down by the Limitation Act 1980 run from the date when the cause of action accrues. In a few cases this date is determined by the Act itself but usually the issue is governed by the general law. The plaintiff's state of knowledge is irrelevant to the accrual of the cause of action. However, not all limitation periods run from the date of accrual, and the time when the plaintiff acquires knowledge of certain matters can be the starting point in personal injury claims, negligence actions and certain other cases.

A cause of action consists of every fact which must be established for the plaintiff to succeed. The definition given by Lord Esher MR in *Read* v *Brown* (1888) is often cited. He said that a cause of action is "every fact which it would be necessary for the plaintiff to prove, if traversed, in order to support his right to the judgment of the Court". In *Cartledge* v *E Jopling & Sons Ltd* (1963) Lord Pearce preferred the definition propounded in *Williams* v *Milotin* (1957), a decision of the High Court of Australia. This was that the term meant "the essential ingredients in the title to the right which it is proposed to enforce". The cause of action therefore accrues at the moment when the factual state of affairs is such as to entitle the plaintiff to judgment. This requires a plaintiff capable of suing and a defendant capable of being sued. It follows that a cause of action does not accrue in favour of or against the administrator of an estate until a grant of representation is taken out, since unlike an executor he has no title until then (*Ingall* v *Moran* (1944)). The Limitation Act 1980 s 26 creates an exception in the case of actions to recover land. For the purposes of the Act an administrator is treated as claiming as if letters of administration had been taken out at the moment of the death.

A cause of action may accrue even though the plaintiff is prevented from suing by a statutory procedural bar, as opposed to the absence of an essential element of the cause of action itself (*Central Electricity Generating Board* v *Halifax Corp* (1962)). In *Coburn* v *Colledge* (1897) it was held that a solicitor's inability to sue for his fees until a month after delivery of his bill did not prevent the limitation period from running during that time. The Solicitors Act 1843 s 37 did not affect the right to payment but merely the procedure for enforcing it. Similarly in *Sevcon Ltd* v *Lucas CAV Ltd* (1986), an action for infringement of patent, the House of Lords held that time ran from the date of the infringement even though the plaintiffs were prevented by the Patents Act 1949 s 13(4) from issuing proceedings at that stage because their application for the patent, though pending, had not been granted. In *Swansea City Council* v *Glass* (1992) the council brought a claim against a landlord under the Housing Act 1957 s 10 for reimbursement of the expenses it had incurred in putting a tenanted house into proper repair. The issue was whether the cause of action accrued only when the council served a written demand for payment as required by the Act. The Court of Appeal held that this requirement was merely procedural and that time therefore ran from the date when the expenses were incurred. Otherwise the local authority could delay the running of time indefinitely simply by refraining from serving the statutory demand. The question whether a requirement laid down in a statute is merely procedural or an inherent element in the cause of action is one of construction. That is no doubt also true of the exact effect of a procedural bar, and a suitably worded provision might permit an action to be stayed pending removal of the bar. However in *Sevcon* v *Lucas* Lord McKay suggested *obiter* that premature proceedings for infringement of patent might be struck out as an abuse of the process of the court. This would render a plaintiff's rights unenforceable altogether if the procedural bar could not be removed within the limitation period.

2. The computation of time

In computing a limitation period which begins on the date when the cause of action accrues, the rest of that day after the moment of accrual is not counted (*Marren* v *Dawson Bentley & Co Ltd* (1961), *Pritam Kaur* v *S Russell & Sons Ltd* (1973)). Thus a personal injury claim in respect of an accident on 10 January 1993 will be in time under LA 1980 s 11(4)(a) if started on or before 10 January 1996. No doubt the same would be true of the date of the plaintiff's knowledge where that is the starting point for a time limit. However the reasoning does not apply where the cause of action accrues at the first moment of a day, for here the plaintiff has the whole of that day in which to issue his action and the principle is that parts of a day are disregarded (*Gelmini* v *Moriggia* (1913)). Thus where a contract debt is payable at any time on 9 January 1993, the cause of action accrues at the first moment of 10 January and time therefore expires on 9 January 1999. If the final day of the limitation period is not a working day for the court office, the plaintiff will nevertheless be in time if he commences the proceedings on the next working day (*Pritam Kaur* v *Russell*). Proceedings are commenced when process is issued. A writ is issued when it is sealed by the court (RSC O 6 r 7(3)). There is no requirement for the proceedings to be *served* within the limitation period.

Once time is running it does so continuously, even during a period when there is no plaintiff who can sue or defendant who can be sued (*Rhodes* v *Smethurst* (1838)). Time is therefore not interrupted by the death of one of the potential parties. In particular the death intestate of a potential defendant does not have the effect of suspending the running of time until an administrator is appointed to his estate. Time does not run against a creditor for the purposes of bankruptcy or company liquidation after the relevant order or resolution but this rule has no effect on matters outside the bankruptcy (*Re Benzon* (1914)).

3. Extensions and suspensions of time

Special provision is made for cases of disability and for cases of fraud, concealment and mistake; see Chapter 12. Infancy and unsoundness of mind are disabilities for these purposes. Acknowledgements and part payments by potential defendants may cause the limitation period to run afresh; see Chapter 4, page 22 and Chapter 9, page 69. The court has a discretion to extend or disapply the limitation period in defamation actions (Chapter 5, page 25) and personal injury claims (Chapter 7, page 50).

At common law a wartime alien enemy could not sue, with the result that time could not run against him, though it could run in his favour. A prisoner of war detained abroad was not subject to any theoretical disability but in practice could not start an action. The position is now governed by the Limitation (Enemies and War Prisoners) Act 1945, which suspends the running of time in certain circumstances.

4. Variations by agreement or estoppel

(a) Contract terms

A contract term may purport to lengthen or shorten the period of limitation either for a claim for breach of the contract itself or for some cause of action arising independently. Actions for breach of contract must normally be brought within six years of the date of the breach (LA 1980 s 5).

(i) Terms shortening the period

A contract clause which stipulates that an action must be brought within a specified time is *prima facie* valid, since the general rule is that the content of the contract is for the parties to decide. But in certain circumstances such clauses will be rendered ineffective by statute. In particular the Unfair Contract Terms Act 1977 will often have that result in cases of business liability as defined in s 1(3). By s 13(1)(a) the Act applies to a contractual limitation period in the same way as to a clause purporting to exclude liability. Other regulatory provisions are the Misrepresentation Act 1967 s 3, the Defective Premises Act 1972 s 6(3) and the Road Traffic Act 1988 s 149.

(ii) Terms lengthening the period

A term providing for a period longer than six years is valid (*Walters* v *Thanet* (1842)). Such terms seem to displace the Limitation Act altogether so that a plea of limitation will simply be ineffective (*Lubovsky* v *Snelling* (1944)). The inconvenient alternative would be a fresh action by the plaintiff for the defendant's breach of contract in pleading the statute.

A contract may sometimes be drafted in such a way that a cause of action will accrue at a relatively late stage. That would be the effect of a clause in a building contract obliging the builder to rectify defects of which he is notified within a specified period after completion of the work. The practical result would be to permit an action to recover losses caused by a breach of contract occurring more than six years earlier. Indemnity covenants will often have a similar result as, for example, in *RH Green & Silley Weir* v *British Railways Board* (1985). The reasons are explained in Chapter 4; see page 20. In addition a limitation period of twelve years (under LA 1980 s 8) will apply where the contract is under seal.

(b) Statements in negotiations

Where the defendant gives an assurance supported by consideration that he will not raise the defence of limitation, it will be enforceable as a matter of contract (*Lubovsky* v *Snelling*). The consideration might take the form of an agreement not to issue proceedings for a certain period or to give a certain number of weeks' notice before doing so.

An assurance by a defendant which is not supported by consideration will normally be enforceable by estoppel, and this possibility seems to be acknowledged by LA 1980 s 13(3). Other statements or actions in the course of negotiations may have a similar effect. In *Kammin's Ballrooms Co Ltd* v *Zenith Investments (Torquay) Ltd* (1971) Lord Diplock stated that the ordinary principles of estoppel apply in this context. There are two main possibilities, namely promissory estoppel and estoppel in the strict sense based on a representation of existing fact. Estoppel by convention may also apply (*The August Leonhardt* (1985)). The term "waiver" is used in some of the cases. If the defendant simply refrains altogether from raising the limitation defence he can no doubt be said to have waived it, but otherwise the expression seems to be used as if it were synonymous with estoppel or at least with certain aspects of it. This is supported by Lord Diplock's comments in *Kammin's Ballrooms Co* v *Zenith Investments*.

Promissory estoppel is relevant to a defendant's statement that limitation will not be pleaded, since this is a matter of intention and not fact. In spite of a lack of case law there can be no doubt that where a defendant has given a clear assurance towards the end of the limitation period that the defence will not be raised and the plaintiff has relied on it by refraining from starting proceedings until time has expired, the doctrine will defeat the plea of limitation; otherwise the plaintiff cannot be restored to his original position. In other circumstances the position is not so clear. The effect of the estoppel depends on what is equitable and it often operates only to suspend rights. A withdrawal of the promise well before the end of the limitation period might therefore be treated as effective. Even after expiry of the period a defendant could presumably resume his rights on giving reasonable notice, as otherwise the claim would never become barred at all.

In *Lubovsky* v *Snelling* a claim by a widow under the Fatal Accidents Act 1846 on behalf of herself and one other person, an admission of liability was held to import a promise not to plead limitation and the implied promise was held enforceable as a contract. However it is clear that an admission of liability would not prevent a plea of limitation in the great majority of damages claims. There would usually be no justification for inferring a promise not to raise the defence as it will not even have accrued at the time. The agreement ought to fail as a contract in any case since no consideration is supplied by the plaintiff. Neither would it normally give rise to a promissory estoppel. A clear and unequivocal assurance is a prerequisite for that doctrine since its effect is to diminish a person's rights without recompense. In *The Sauria* (1957) the Court of Appeal criticised *Lubovsky* v *Snelling* along these lines and distinguished it on the basis that it had been an essential part of the agreement that, as the insurance company's representative had stated at the time, proceedings would need to be commenced even if quantum was agreed because the court would have to approve the settlement and apportion the damages between the two claimants. An admission of liability in a claim for unliquidated damages will therefore normally have no effect for limitation purposes. But in a claim for a liquidated sum it will no doubt be a sufficient acknowledgement for the purposes of LA 1980 s 29(5) and therefore cause time to run afresh; see Chapter 4, page 22.

It need hardly be said that a plaintiff's solicitor should not rely on anything less than an unambiguous promissory assurance. The fact that negotiations are continuing is insufficient. Neither will a mere misunderstanding between the parties suffice (*The August Leonhardt*). In that case the defendants' conduct was not open to criticism in any way, but it is clear from the decision that matters might well be different where the defendant or his representatives are responsible for the plaintiff's mistaken belief. As already mentioned, a clear promise or representation is a prerequisite for promissory estoppel, but on suitable facts estoppel by convention may prevent the defendant from denying that a promise not to plead limitation was made. The promise thus established may then become enforceable by promissory estoppel since there is no reason why the two forms of estoppel should not operate together.

(c) *Statements before negotiations*

In *Kaliszewska* v *John Clague & Partners* (1984) the plaintiff sued an architect for negligence in the design of her bungalow. Cracks first appeared in 1974, about four years after completion of the building. The defendant made an inspection and told the plaintiff that she had nothing to worry about. The cracks were filled in and the plaintiff took no further action. In late 1976 further cracks appeared and the floors began to subside. Other expert advice was obtained in 1978 and extensive work carried out in 1980. The writ was issued in 1982. The defendant denied negligence and pleaded the limitation period. The court held that the cause of action accrued in January 1971 at the latest but that the defence of limitation could not succeed because of the defendant's advice to the plaintiff in 1974. He had in effect told her then that the bungalow was not damaged or defective in any significant way; that was untrue. She relied on the advice to her detriment by not pursuing the matter at that stage. The defendant was therefore estopped from pleading the time bar. The judge did not go into detail on the precise effect of the estoppel. He merely said that estoppel would not have availed the plaintiff if she had allowed more than six years to elapse from the date when she discovered the truth. Since that had been in 1978 the writ was in time.

The case is of course an example of estoppel by representation of fact; there was nothing promissory in the defendant's advice of 1974. This form of estoppel might be relevant, in theory at least, to any type of claim and applies even where the representation is entirely innocent. It has potential value in cases where the parties continue to deal with each other after accrual of the cause of action. The same reasoning was applied in *Westlake* v *Bracknell District Council* (1987).

(d) Extinction of the cause of action

What has been said so far in this chapter applies where the time limit in question merely bars the remedy. Matters may be different in the few cases where the effect of the expiry of time is to extinguish the cause of action itself; see Chapter 15, page 109. In such a case the bar is not merely procedural but goes to the very validity of the claim. It is then one in respect of a cause of action which does not exist and it is generally accepted that estoppel cannot operate to create fresh rights. This reasoning obviously does not apply to an action on a contract not to plead the statute, should one be found to exist.

Chapter 4

Contract

1. General principles

The Limitation Act 1980 s 5 provides that an action founded on simple contract is subject to a limitation period of six years running from the date when the cause of action accrues. The expression "simple contract" is not defined but clearly includes a contract which is not in the form of a deed. Where the contract is under seal the period is twelve years under s 8 since such a contract is an example of a specialty; see Chapter 11, page 78. A contract made by a deed executed without a seal under the Law of Property (Miscellaneous Provisions) Act 1989 s 1 is presumably within s 8 rather than s 5. Contractual terms varying the length of the limitation period are *prima facie* valid. These are discussed in Chapter 3; see page 13. Where the right to a sum of money payable under a contract has become barred by the statute, any right to interest accruing, even in the six years before action, is also barred (*Elder* v *Northcott* (1930)).

The cause of action accrues when the breach of contract is committed, even if the plaintiff has not then suffered any loss (*Battley* v *Faulkner* (1820), *Lynn* v *Bamber* (1930)). It makes no difference that the existence of the breach or of the loss is not reasonably discoverable when it occurs. The reforms of the Latent Damage Act 1986 do not apply to contract actions (see Chapter 6, page 34), though if there is fraud, concealment or mistake LA 1980 s 32 will have a broadly similar effect (see Chapter 12, page 84). Determination of the date of breach will often involve questions of construction of the contract. The contractual duty and the time for its performance must be ascertained. Unless the contract provides otherwise, payment for goods sold or services rendered becomes due on delivery of the goods or on completion of the work, and time therefore runs from that moment. Where there is a contractual warranty that a particular state of affairs exists, the issue is the time when according to the terms of the contract matters must be as warranted. In the case of the terms implied in a contract for the sale of goods by the Sale of Goods Act 1979 s 14, this is the time of delivery. Where several breaches of contract occur, each gives rise to a fresh cause of action. The assignment of a debt will not have that effect since the assignee can be in no better position than the assignor. The same applies to rights acquired by subrogation. However, a novation involves a new contract and a breach of it will of course create a new cause of action (*Chatsworth Investment Ltd* v *Cussins (Contractors) Ltd* (1969)).

By LA 1980 s 36(1) the time limits of s 5 and s 8 do not apply to a claim for an injunction, specific performance or other equitable relief except in so far as they may be applied by analogy in equity. Section 36(2) preserves the equitable jurisdiction to refuse relief on the grounds of acquiescence or laches. These matters are discussed in Chapter 2; see page 4. By LA 1980 s 39 the Act has no application at all to any action or arbitration for which a period of limitation is prescribed by or under any other enactment. Various statutes relating to international transport are in this category. They are also discussed in Chapter 2; see page 6.

In certain circumstances a breach of contract may render the defendant liable in both contract and tort. In particular the breach of a contractual duty to take reasonable care often gives rise also to a cause of action in negligence; see Chapter 5, page 26. This is significant because the cause of action in negligence accrues only at the date of the damage, which may be a lot later than the time of the negligent act (see Chapter 6, page 28), and secondly because the Latent Damage Act 1986 does not apply to contractual claims, as already mentioned.

2. Particular instances

(a) Omissions

There may be difficulty where the defendant's breach of contract consists of a failure to act. In *Midland Bank Trust Co Ltd* v *Hett, Stubbs & Kemp* (1979) an option to purchase a farm was granted in 1961 but was not registered under the Land Charges Act 1925 by the defendants, a firm of solicitors, with the result that their client lost the right to buy the land when it was sold to another person in 1967. The option should have been registered on its creation in 1961, but registration at any time before the sale would have been effective. Oliver J held that the solicitors' duty to register the option continued until it was performed or until effective performance became impossible on the eventual sale of the land. It followed that "it was then that the contract was broken once and for all" so that the contractual cause of action was not statute-barred in 1972 when proceedings were issued.

Obviously that approach depends on the existence of a continuing contractual duty. It was not adopted by the Court of Appeal in *Bell* v *Peter Browne & Co* (1990). The defendants, also a firm of solicitors, acted for the husband in divorce proceedings. It was agreed that the matrimonial home should be put into the wife's sole name but the husband was to have a one-sixth share of the eventual proceeds of sale. A transfer to the wife was completed but the defendants failed to take any steps to protect their client's interest. This should have been done through a trust deed or mortgage executed by the wife and through the registration of a caution against the title to make the husband's rights enforceable against a purchaser from the wife. The mortgage or declaration of trust needed to be contemporaneous with the transfer itself, but the solicitors could have lodged a caution at any time before the eventual sale. It might have been effective on its own, though that depended on the operation of the doctrine of part performance. Eight years later the house was sold. The wife spent the entire proceeds and the husband sued the solicitors for his loss. The issue was whether the cause of action accrued at or around the time of the transfer, or alternatively at the time of the sale by the wife. The plaintiff relied on *Midland Bank Trust Co Ltd* v *Hett, Stubbs & Kemp* but was unsuccessful. The Court of Appeal held that the solicitors' contractual duty was to register the caution as soon as reasonably practicable after the transfer. Their failure to do so was a breach of contract at that stage and the limitation period therefore started to run then, with the result that the action was out of time. The fact that the breach was capable of being remedied made no difference. A remediable breach was just as much a breach when it occurred as an irremediable breach and the subsequent failure to make good the omission did not itself amount to a further breach; if it did, the effect would be to frustrate the purpose of the Limitation Act. A continuing contractual obligation would of course have different consequences, since in such a case there is a fresh breach on each successive day. Whether a duty was a continuing one or not was a question of construction of the contract but the view of the Court of Appeal was that such duties would be exceptional. The normal repairing covenant in a tenancy agreement was given as an example but the duties owed by the defendant solicitors to the plaintiff were not in that category.

Midland Bank Trust Co Ltd v *Hett, Stubbs & Kemp* was distinguished by Nichols LJ on the ground that there the solicitors had continued to have dealings with their client in relation to the option and therefore were never *functi officio*. It is true that Oliver J attached some weight to the fact that the solicitors were consulted by their client on several occasions over the six and a half years between the making of the option agreement and the sale of the land. Nevertheless it is likely that a claim on similar facts would be decided differently today. Beldam LJ was "not persuaded" that the case could be distinguished at all from the situation in *Bell* v *Peter Browne*. The correct approach therefore involves identifying the contractual duty which has been broken and the time by which performance is due. The contract action will become statute-barred six years thereafter, unless on the true construction of the contract the duty is a continuing one. However an action in tort may be possible even outside that period, and *Bell* v *Peter Browne* is considered further in Chapter 6; see page 32.

(b) Anticipatory breach

Anticipatory breach occurs when a party repudiates some or all of his contractual obligations before performance is due by making it plain through words or conduct that when the time for performance comes he will not or cannot perform. In spite of the name, anticipatory breach alone does not create a cause of action. The plaintiff may ignore the repudiation and the issue is then simply whether or not proper performance is actually rendered when the time comes (*White & Carter (Councils) Ltd* v *McGregor* (1962)). Alternatively he may accept the repudiation as a termination of the contract. His right to do so will depend on the seriousness of the threatened breach and the nature of the contractual obligation in question. Where the right exists, its exercise gives the plaintiff the right to sue immediately. The cause of action therefore accrues at the time of the plaintiff's termination of the contract (*Hochster* v *De la Tour* (1853)).

(c) Indemnity contracts

The right to sue for an indemnity does not accrue until the existence and amount of the liability against which indemnity is sought have been established by a judgment, arbitration award or settlement (*County & District Properties* v *Jenner* (1974), *Post Office* v *Norwich Union Fire Insurance Society Ltd* (1967), *Bradley* v *Eagle Star Insurance Co Ltd* (1989)). The cause of action may in fact accrue after this time if the terms of the contract lay down some further requirement, for example that the right should arise only when the party to be indemnified has himself satisfied the liability. But it cannot accrue at any earlier time. An advance repudiation of his obligations by the indemnor would be an anticipatory breach but no more. Consequently no cause of action at all would accrue unless the repudiation were accepted by the innocent party, and any such acceptance would give him only a right to damages. To obtain an indemnity as such, he would have to elect to treat the contract as continuing.

(d) Loans

The right to sue on a loan accrues on the date stipulated by the contract for repayment. If the contract is silent on this point or if it merely requires payment on demand, the common law rule was that time ran from the date of the loan itself (*Reeves* v *Butcher* (1891), *Re Brown's Estate* (1893)). The position in such cases is now governed by LA 1980 s 6, which provides that time will begin to run under s 5 only when a written demand for repayment is made by or on behalf of the creditor, or any one of them where there are joint creditors. This does not apply where the debtor enters into any collateral obligation to pay the debt or any part of it which is effective to make payment due by an ascertainable date or on demand (s 6(2)).

Money held by a bank or building society for a customer, whether in a current account or on deposit, constitutes a loan. In the absence of anything to the contrary in the banking contract a demand by the customer is a condition precedent to repayment, and time therefore does not run against him until then. This was the rule even before LA 1980 s 6 (*Joachimson* v *Swiss Bank Corp* (1921), *Arab Bank* v *Barclays Bank* (1954), *Atkinson* v *Bradford Third Equitable Benefit Society* (1890)). An action for repayment of a sum wrongly debited by a bank is on the same basis, and the limitation period under s 5 therefore runs from the date of the customer's demand and not the date of the debit (*National Bank of Commerce* v *National Westminster Bank* (1990)). Overdrafts and other advances to customers are of course also loans. If the banking contract is not effective to fix a date for repayment, the common law rule was that no demand was necessary and the bank's right to recover was therefore barred six years after the last advance (*Parr's Banking Co Ltd* v *Yates* (1898)). The position has now been altered by LA 1980 s 6 in the way already described so that a demand is now needed before time runs.

(e) Negotiable instruments

Where a promissory note or bill of exchange contains provisions determining the time for payment, the cause of action accrues at that time. But if no such time is specified the limitation period runs from the date of the instrument or of its delivery if later. The same applies to a note or bill expressed simply to be repayable on demand; no demand is in fact necessary (*Norton* v *Ellam* (1837)).

(f) Guarantees

(i) The creditor's cause of action against the surety accrues when the surety becomes liable under the terms of the contract of guarantee (*Colvin* v *Buckle* (1841)). This may be the date of default by the principal debtor, but it is always a question of construction of the contract. If payment by the surety is expressed to be due on demand the common law rule applicable to loans and negotiable instruments does not apply and so no liability arises until demand is actually made (*Re Brown's Estate* (1893), *Bradford Old Bank* v *Sutcliffe* (1918)). Where the creditor's rights against the debtor become statute-barred, the liability of the surety is not necessarily affected as it depends on his own breach of the contract of guarantee, and therefore time may run against him from a later date than against the debtor (*Carter* v *White* (1883)). Interest falling due in the six years before action may be recoverable against the surety even though his liability for the principal sum has become statute-barred, as long as failure to pay the interest constitutes a fresh breach of the guarantee on its true construction (*Parr's Banking Co Ltd* v *Yates* 1898)).

(ii) The surety's rights against the debtor will depend on the terms of their contract but in the normal case the right to be indemnified by the debtor will accrue at the time of the surety's payment to the creditor (*Davies* v *Humphreys* (1840), *Angrove* v *Tippett* (1865)). A separate such right accrues with each payment by the surety. Since the surety can be liable to the creditor even after the creditor's remedy against the debtor is barred, the surety's right of indemnity may render the debt effectively enforceable for a time after expiry of the limitation period. But a surety who pays a debt which has become statute-barred as against him cannot recover from the debtor (*Re Morris* (1922)).

(iii) The surety's right to contribution from his co-surety is considered in Chapter 11; see page 76.

(g) Solicitors' undertakings

A solicitor's undertaking supported by consideration is enforceable as a contract and LA 1980 s 5 applies in the normal way to such an action. Whether there is consideration or not, an undertaking is enforceable in certain ways through the exercise of the High Court's supervisory jurisdiction over solicitors. No limitation period applies though the lapse of time is a factor relevant in the exercise of the court's discretion (*Bray* v *Stuart A. West & Co* (1989)).

(h) Quasi-contract

Although LA 1980 s 5 is expressed to apply to actions founded on simple contract, it seems that it also governs quasi-contractual claims (*Re Diplock* (1948), *Chesworth* v *Farrar* (1967)). In the case of an action to recover benefits conferred under a mistake of fact s 32 will apply and the limitation period will not run until the plaintiff has discovered the mistake or could with reasonable diligence have done so; see Chapter 12, page 84.

3. Acknowledgements and part-payments

The Limitation Act 1980 s 29(5) provides that where the defendant acknowledges a debt or other liquidated pecuniary claim or makes a part-payment of it, the plaintiff's right of action is treated as accruing at the time of the acknowledgement or payment. The limitation period therefore commences afresh. But a part-payment of interest due does not extend the time for claiming the remainder of the interest; instead it is treated for these purposes as payment in respect of the principal debt (s 29(6)). By s 29(7) the limitation period may be repeatedly extended in this way by further acknowledgements or payments. However the same subsection also provides that an acknowledgement or part-payment cannot operate to revive a right of action once it has become barred by the Act. The acknowledgement or payment must therefore be made during the currency of the limitation period then applicable. By s 31(6) an acknowledgement binds the acknowledgor and his successors, as defined in s 31(9), but no other person, and by s 31(7) a part-payment binds all those who are liable in respect of the claim. These provisions are particularly important in the context of guarantees.

For these purposes an acknowledgement must be in writing and signed by the person making it (s 30(1)). Section 30(2) provides that an acknowledgement or part-payment by an agent of the debtor will be effective but also that any acknowledgement or part-payment must be made to the creditor or his agent; a document directed to another party will not suffice. Beyond this the Act does not define the term "acknowledgement". A copy of a company's balance sheet signed by the directors and referring to the debt will qualify provided that it is actually received by the creditor or his agent (*Jones* v *Bellgrove Properties* (1949), *Re Compania de Electricidad de la Provincia de Buenos Aires Ltd* (1980)). A refusal to pay, as opposed to a denial of liability, may also suffice (*Good* v *Parry* (1963)). The statutory provisions do not apply to unliquidated claims but a claim for a *quantum meruit* does come within them (*Amantilla Ltd* v *Telefusion plc* (1987)).

Chapter 5

Tort

This and the three chapters which follow are concerned chiefly with tort actions. By the Limitation Act 1980 s 2 these are normally subject to a limitation period of six years from the date when the cause of action accrues. This chapter deals with accrual of the cause of action (though the detail in negligence actions is left to Chapter 6), the particular rules applicable to defamation and conversion and the possibility of concurrent liability in contract and tort. Negligence actions and the Latent Damage Act 1986 are discussed in Chapter 6. Personal injury claims and the Consumer Protection Act 1987 are explained in Chapters 7 and 8.

1. Accrual of the cause of action

In the cases of the few torts which are actionable *per se* the cause of action accrues at the time of the wrongful act. In other instances there is no cause of action until damage occurs. Libel and certain types of slander are actionable *per se*, as is the tort of trespass. Conversion is also actionable *per se*, though normally the plaintiff would in any event suffer damage at the time of the wrongful act. Negligence and breach of statutory duty are actionable only on proof of damage and the same applies to public nuisance. Private nuisance to an easement or *profit à prendre* is actionable *per se* (*Nicholls* v *Ely Beet Sugar Factory Ltd* (1936)). In other instances of private nuisance damage is in theory a requirement but is often presumed. Damage is also necessary for a successful action in the tort of deceit but here the question of accrual of the cause of action loses its importance in any event because of the application of LA 1980 s 32, discussed in Chapter 12.

The repetition of a single tortious act, such as a second publication of defamatory material, will of course give rise to a second cause of action, even though the first may be statute-barred. Similarly a fresh cause of action accrues from day to day in the case of a continuing tort and the plaintiff can therefore sue in respect of the six years before commencement of the proceedings but not any earlier time. The onus is on the defendant to show what part of the damage occurred before the statutory period (*Clarkson* v *Modern Foundries Ltd* (1957)). A continuing nuisance is an example of this sort of case for in nuisance a new cause of action accrues whenever further damage occurs (*Darley Main Colliery Co* v *Mitchell* (1886)). Similarly an ongoing trespass to land, which is actionable *per se*, gives rise to a fresh cause of action from day to day.

In other instances the normal rule is that the occurrence of a second item of damage as a result of the breach of duty does not create a second cause of action (*Fetter* v *Beale* (1701), *Cartledge* v *E Jopling & Sons* (1963)). There are two exceptions to this. First, two causes of action exist where two distinct rights of the plaintiff have been infringed, for example by an act causing both personal injuries and property damage (*Brunsden* v *Humphrey* (1884)). Secondly, in torts actionable only on proof of damage a later item of damage will give rise to a fresh cause of action if it is distinct from the original damage (*Mount Albert BC* v *Johnson* (1979)). Where there have been more than one item of damage, the courts have nearly always proceeded on the basis of a single cause of action.

2. Defamation

Libel is actionable *per se* and the cause of action therefore accrues at the time of publication of the defamatory material. A second publication gives rise to a second cause of action. Slander is actionable *per se* when it consists of the imputation of a contagious disease, or of a criminal offence punishable with imprisonment, or of unchastity on the part of a woman or girl (Slander of Women Act 1891 s 1), or of unfitness or incompetence on the part of the plaintiff in his or her work or business. In other cases of slander the cause of action accrues only when special damage is suffered.

Under LA 1980 s 4A the limitation period is three years, though where the plaintiff's failure to sue is because facts relevant to the cause of action did not become known to him within that time, s 32A permits the action to be started within a year of his eventual discovery of those facts provided that leave of the High Court is obtained. Sections 4A and 32A were inserted by the Administration of Justice Act 1985. The extension of time under s 32A is not available where the cause of action accrued before 30 December 1985. The section provides no guidance on what facts are relevant to the cause of action for this purpose nor on the circumstances in which leave is likely to be granted.

3. Conversion

Prima facie LA 1980 s 2 applies and therefore the limitation period is six years from the time of the wrongful act. Additional provisions are contained in ss 3 and 4. Provided no theft is involved their effect is as follows:

(*a*) Where the plaintiff has not recovered possession of the goods within the limitation period, his title is extinguished by s 3(2). The statute therefore bars both the remedy and the right in this particular case and so it is not open to the plaintiff to recover the goods by non-judicial means. Neither can he sue in respect of any subsequent wrongful dealings with them.

(*b*) By s 3(1), where a further conversion of the goods takes place before the plaintiff recovers possession, the limitation period in respect of the further conversion runs from the time of the first conversion.

Thus if a chattel is converted in year one by A, and sold by him in year four to B, B will acquire title in year seven and from that point both he and A will have a limitation defence in an action by the original owner.

There are different provisions in respect of cases of theft, which is given an extended definition for these purposes by s 4(5). The effect of s 4 is as follows:

(*a*) Time does not run at all in favour of the thief or any person claiming through him otherwise than by a purchase made in good faith. Thus a thief or a receiver (or donee) from the thief will remain liable indefinitely, even if the plaintiff's title is later extinguished.

(*b*) A bona fide purchaser for value of the stolen property is entitled to rely on the defence of limitation but the period runs only from the time of his purchase. Any subsequent converter, including a thief, will be in the same position if sued by the true owner. In either case the rules contained in s 3 apply. It should be remembered that in certain circumstances a bona fide purchaser for value may acquire good title (and a defence to a conversion action) under an exception to the rule *nemo dat quod non habet*. The position is rather complicated and an example may clarify matters. If after a theft from A in year one the stolen goods are acquired by B, a bona fide purchaser for value, in year eight, sold by him to C in year ten and stolen from C by D in year twelve, B C and D will all be able to plead limitation from year fourteen in any action by A. At the same time C will acquire title under s 3(2). His claim against D is subject to no time limit and the same is true of A's rights of action against the original thief and any other converters before the purchase by B.

4. Concurrent liability in contract and tort

Although the limitation period is six years in both contract (by LA 1980 s 5) and the tort of negligence (by s 2), there are nevertheless two important differences between them for limitation purposes. The first is that in contract the cause of action accrues immediately on the breach of duty whereas in negligence there is no cause of action until damage results. The second is that the Latent Damage Act 1986 does not apply to a contract action; see Chapter 6, page 34. The consequence is that the limitation period can be much more generous in negligence. In certain instances careless conduct constituting a breach of a contractual duty to take reasonable care, usually the result of an implied term of the contract, can give rise to liability in both contract and tort at the same time, with the result that an action in negligence may succeed even when the contract claim on the same facts has become barred. The main contractual relationships where this concurrent liability exists are employer and employee, carrier and passenger, occupier of premises and visitor, bailor and bailee and professional person and client. In personal injury claims the existence of dual liability is not significant because they are all subject to LA 1980 ss 11–14, but it may be crucial in an action against a professional such as a solicitor, accountant or surveyor.

For some time it was considered that a professional person's liability to his client was purely contractual (*Groom* v *Crocker* (1938) (solicitor), *Bagot* v *Stevens Scanlan & Co* (1966) (architect)). Then in 1976 it was held in *Esso Petroleum Co* v *Mardon* that a careless statement could result in liability for negligence and for breach of a collateral warranty. This decision was relied on in *Midland Bank Trust Co* v *Hett, Stubbs & Kemp* (1978), where notwithstanding *Groom* v *Crocker* it was held that a solicitor owed duties to his client in both contract and tort. This was assumed to be correct in *Forster* v *Oughtred & Co* (1982), *Baker* v *Ollard & Bentley* (1982) and *D W Moore & Co* v *Ferrier* (1988). More recently the courts have become wary of rather uncontrolled expansion in the law of tort and there has been a tendency to say that where parties have chosen to define their obligations by contract there is no room for the imposition of more extensive duties through the law of tort. In *Tai Hing Cotton Mill* v *Liu Chong Hing Bank* (1986), a Privy Council case which concerned the relationship of bank and customer, Lord Scarman discouraged the search for tortious liability in circumstances where the parties are in a contractual relationship. It was "correct in principle and necessary for the avoidance of confusion in the law to adhere to the contractual analysis".

In subsequent cases involving solicitors the Court of Appeal has accepted the existence of concurrent liability, though not without expressing doubts over its desirability, as for example in *Lee* v *Thompson* (Lloyd LJ) and *Bell* v *Peter Browne & Co* (Mustill LJ). On the other hand there was some support for the present position from the House of Lords in *Caparo Industries* v *Dickman* (1990) and *Murphy* v *Brentwood District Council* (1990). Cases involving other professions have been approached in the same way (*Pirelli General Cable Works* v *Oscar Faber & Partners* (1983) (engineers), *Thake* v *Maurice* (1986) (doctors), *Iron Trade Mutual Insurance Co Ltd* v *JK Buckenham* (1990) and *Islander Trucking Ltd* v *Hogg Robinson & Gardner Mountain (Marine) Ltd* (1990) (insurance brokers)).

It is clear from *D & F Estates Ltd* v *Church Commissioners for England* (1988) and *Murphy* v *Brentwood District Council* that the tortious duty of those involved in construction or manufacturing industries with respect to defective or damaged property is narrow in its scope and certainly not coextensive with any contractual duty of care; see Chapter 6, page 28. However, in other contexts the position is different, and as the law stands at present a plaintiff whose contractual cause of action is out of time will often be able to sue successfully in tort.

Chapter 6

Negligence actions and the Latent Damage Act 1986

This chapter deals first with the question of accrual of the cause of action in negligence cases and secondly with the Latent Damage Act 1986. That Act is not entirely confined to latent damage cases. The fifteen year long-stop of LA 1980 s 14B, inserted by the 1986 Act, applies (in addition to s 2) in all negligence actions except personal injury claims; see page 37.

1. Accrual of the cause of action

(a) General principles

The cause of action in negligence accrues when the plaintiff suffers damage going beyond the merely trivial. Thus in a personal injury claim the relevant time is when the plaintiff suffers injury which is not insignificant, even if he has no reason to suspect that it has occurred (*Cartledge* v *E Jopling & Sons Ltd* (1963)). Similarly in a property damage case the cause of action accrues when the damage is sustained, whether or not it is discoverable by the plaintiff at that stage (*Pirelli General Cable Works Ltd* v *Oscar Faber & Partners* (1983)). In that case the House of Lords rejected the reasoning of the Court of Appeal in *Sparham-Souter* v *Town & Country Developments (Essex) Ltd* (1976) that the cause of action accrued only when building damage became apparent because until then the plaintiff could sell the property without loss. Where the damage to the plaintiff genuinely takes the form of economic loss, the cause of action accrues when that loss is incurred. Again the state of the plaintiff's knowledge is irrelevant. The harshness of the rule in cases where the damage is latent has been largely removed by legislation in personal injury claims and negligence claims but the time of accrual of the cause of action remains relevant and the statutory reforms do not alter the applicable legal rules.

(b) Damaged or defective buildings and chattels

The decision in *Pirelli* also established that no cause of action accrues simply because the plaintiff's property is rendered defective by the defendant's carelessness. Thus the alleged negligence of consulting engineers causing a defect to be incorporated into the structure of a chimney could not create a cause of action on the completion of the work but only when the defect resulted in physical damage, namely cracks in the chimney. Exceptionally, according to Lord Fraser who gave the leading speech in *Pirelli*, a defect might be so gross that the building is "doomed from the start", in which case the owner's cause of action will accrue as soon as it is built. This would of course be a right to sue for pure economic loss, no physical damage as such having yet occurred. This exception has seldom been applied, and since the decision in *Murphy* v *Brentwood District Council* (1990), mentioned below, it presumably has little or no further part to play. Although *Pirelli* is unquestioned authority for the basic rule that the cause of action in property damage cases accrues on the occurrence of the damage, various points need to be made about the case.

(*i*) Since the decisions of the House of Lords in *D & F Estates Ltd* v *Church Commissioners for England* (1988) and *Murphy* v *Brentwood District Council* the basic position is that negligence in the construction of a building will not give rise to any right of action in tort (except under the Defective Premises Act 1972), unless it results in physical injury to persons or to property other than the building itself. A defect or damage to the building will not suffice even if it creates a risk of physical injury and even if the building is "doomed from the start". These are examples of pure economic loss. The same reasoning applies to the manufacturer of a chattel. It ought to follow that there should have been no tortious cause of action in *Pirelli* itself, as the only damage was to the chimney of the building. In *Murphy* v *Brentwood District Council* Lord Keith stated that the case is to be regarded as an example of liability under *Hedley Byrne & Co* v *Heller & Partners* (1964), which may permit the recovery of economic loss caused by negligent advice. But if it is an example of economic loss, the cause of action would accrue at the time of that loss rather than the later time of the physical damage. This was acknowledged by Lord Keith. As explained below (see page 31) economic loss caused by negligent advice would normally be suffered at the time of the plaintiff's reliance on that advice. The advantage of Lord Keith's analysis for the purposes of the restrictive approach to economic loss taken by the House of Lords in *Murphy* v *Brentwood District Council* is that since the *Hedley Byrne* duty is based on ideas of proximity, particularly reliance, it is most unlikely in the context of construction or manufacturing that it would ever be owed to anyone other than the recipient of the advice. Furthermore the recipient would normally have a contract with the defendant anyway and, if so, the tortious duty to avoid economic loss adds nothing. However there is a difference for limitation purposes because although in these circumstances the causes of action in contract and tort will typically accrue at substantially the same time, the Latent Damage Act 1986 can apply only to the negligence claim. These matters are discussed below; see page 31 and page 34.

Further decisions will be needed to clarify the relationship between *Murphy* v *Brentwood DC* and *Pirelli* v *Oscar Faber*. It was considered in *Nitrigin Eireann Teoranta* v *Inco Alloys Ltd* (1992). In 1983 cracks were found in tubing comprised in part of a chemical production plant owned by the plaintiffs. They were not fully aware of the extent of the defects despite reasonable investigation and their repairs were therefore inadequate. In 1984 the tube ruptured and there was an explosion which caused the plant to shut down. The defendants, the manufacturers of the tubing, contended that since it had sustained damage in 1983, more than six years before issue of the writ, the action was out of time. In accordance with *Murphy* v *Brentwood DC* May J held that the damage to the tubing had been pure economic loss not recoverable in negligence and that therefore no cause of action had accrued at that stage. He accepted Lord Keith's explanation of *Pirelli* as an example of tortious liability for economic loss arising from a relationship between the plaintiff and a professional person. But no cause of action had accrued when the economic loss was suffered on the supply of the tubing in 1981, because the defendants were not professional people engaged to advise but simply manufacturers, albeit specialists. Their relationship with the plaintiffs was therefore not of the type which could give rise to liability for economic loss. It followed that the cause of action accrued at the time of the explosion in 1984 when physical damage to property other than the tubing was sustained. This had been less than six years before commencement of the proceedings and the action was therefore not statute-barred.

(*ii*) In *D & F Estates* Lord Bridge raised the possibility that the various elements of a "complex structure" might be regarded as distinct from one another so that damage to one part caused by a defect in another part could be treated as damage to property other than the defective item itself. In *Murphy* this idea was largely rejected but a distinction was drawn between integral parts of the structure and other items such as a central heating boiler or an electrical installation. If such ancillary equipment malfunctions and damages the building, an action in negligence could lie. This is of course a normal application of negligence principles. The cause of action would accrue at the time of the damage.

(*iii*) In *Murphy* Lord Bridge suggested an exception to the rule against recovery in respect of defects or damage in the building itself. Where because of a dangerous defect the building is a potential source of injury to persons or their property on neighbouring land or on the highway, the owner should be able to sue the builder in tort for the cost of such work as is necessary to protect himself from liability to these third parties. In such a case the cause of action would presumably accrue at the time when the defect became dangerous.

(*iv*) Matters are complicated further by the decision in *Junior Books Ltd* v *Veitchi Co Ltd* (1983). This was an action against allegedly negligent sub-contractors for the cost of repairing flooring which they had installed in the plaintiff's premises. Most of the floor was merely defective and not damaged, yet the House of Lords held on a preliminary point that the defendants' duty of care extended to such losses because of the extremely close relationship between the parties. In contrast with the decision in *Pirelli*, the occurrence of physical damage as a result of the defect was not necessary. The cause of action presumably accrued when the work was completed, though the point was not in issue. Like the "doomed from the start" exception to the *Pirelli* rule, *Junior Books* is an example of an action for pure economic loss. The decision has been comprehensively rejected by later courts and though not actually overruled has been limited to its own facts by both the Court of Appeal and the House of Lords, most notably in *D & F Estates*. Like *Pirelli*, it was categorised as an example of *Hedley Byrne* liability by Lord Keith in *Murphy* v *Brentwood District Council*.

(c) *Professional advisers*

When negligence by a professional adviser such as an architect or surveyor causes a building or chattel to become damaged or defective the position is as already described. Where the result is merely economic loss, the cause of action accrues when that loss is suffered. There is some scope for confusing the two types of case in instances involving physical damage to property. The issue is what losses or damage the defendant's negligence actually caused. In *Secretary of State for the Environment* v *Essex, Goodman & Suggitt* (1986) the plaintiffs took a lease of a building in reliance on an allegedly negligent report from the defendants, a firm of surveyors. It was held that the cause of action accrued when the plaintiffs entered into the lease and not at the later date when the building was damaged by the defects which the defendants had failed to discover. The defendants had not caused the defects or the damage; they had caused the plaintiffs the economic loss of entering the lease on terms which did not take account of the property's defective condition. Consequently the action was statute-barred.

The cause of action accrues when the loss is suffered by the plaintiff, whether or not it is discoverable by him at that stage. The issue is one of fact but there seems to be a strong tendency on the part of the courts to treat the cause of action as accruing at the earliest of the possible dates. The crucial moment is usually, though not necessarily, the time when the plaintiff acts in reliance on the negligent advice. In instances where there is a contract between the parties—and that is typically the case—the result is that the cause of action in negligence will normally accrue at the same time as the contractual cause of action or a fairly short time later. This goes some way towards removing the differences between the contractual and the tortious rights.

The facts of the leading cases will illustrate the operation of the rule. In *Forster* v *Oughtred & Co* (1982) the plaintiff had executed a mortgage on her house in 1973 as security for her son's borrowings. In 1975 she had to pay almost £70,000 to the mortgagee. In 1980 she sued her solicitors alleging that they had been negligent in failing to inform her properly of the extent of the liabilities covered by the mortgage. A contractual claim was of course out of time. The Court of Appeal held that any cause of action in negligence accrued in 1973 when the plaintiff executed the mortgage, not in 1975 when she made the payment. The very brief justification for this conclusion was that by executing the mortgage the plaintiff had made her house subject to a greater encumbrance than should have been the case. That was a sufficient loss to give rise to a cause of action in negligence at that stage even though there was no certainty then that she would be called on for any payment at all.

After the decision in *Pirelli*, which drew the distinction between damage and a mere defect, there was some doubt whether the reasoning in *Forster* remained reliable, for it could be said that the defendants' negligence in failing to give proper advice was analogous to the construction of a defective building and that the plaintiff therefore suffered no actual damage until she became obliged to make a payment to the mortgagee. However the courts have in fact continued with the same approach as before. In *D W Moore & Co Ltd* v *Ferrier* (1988) the plaintiff insurance brokers entered an agreement in 1971 with one Fenton under which he became a director and shareholder. The agreement contained a covenant by him purporting to restrict his right to compete with the plaintiffs for a certain period after leaving the company. In 1980 he left and set up as an insurance broker in the locality. The plaintiffs then found that they could not prevent him from doing so because the restrictive covenant had been badly drafted; it applied only if Mr. Fenton ceased to be a member of the company but in fact he retained his shares and therefore remained a member even after giving up his directorship. In 1985 the plaintiffs issued proceedings against the solicitors who had drafted the agreement. They contended that they had incurred no loss until 1980 when the third party set up in business on his own account. However the Court of Appeal held that the cause of action accrued on the signing of the defective agreement in 1971. Again the court's reasoning was far from expansive. The plaintiffs should have had a valid restrictive covenant as part of the arrangements made. That is something of value; it can be assigned to the purchaser of a business. Because of the defendant's negligence, the plaintiffs actually acquired something of lesser value—and the loss was therefore suffered at the time of the 1971 agreement. Its quantification at that stage would have been difficult, but that was a separate matter.

The same approach has been taken in other cases involving solicitors, for example *Baker* v *Ollard & Bentley* (1982) and *Lee* v *Thompson* (1989). By contrast, the conclusion of Oliver J on this issue in *Midland Bank Trust Co Ltd* v *Hett, Stubbs & Kemp* (see page 18) was that the damage occurred only when the land which was the subject matter of the option that the defendant solicitors had failed to register was eventually sold. But that case seems very much out of line with other decisions and did not commend itself to the Court of Appeal in *Bell* v *Peter Browne & Co* (see page 18). There the Court of Appeal held that the cause of action in tort accrued at or very soon after the time when the matrimonial home was put into the wife's sole name without any steps for the protection of the husband's share in the proceeds of sale, rather than several years later when the wife sold the property and spent the proceeds. While unprotected, the husband's equitable interest was of less value than it would have been if proper steps had been taken, and the husband would have been disadvantaged by the solicitors' omission in any attempt to enforce his interest against either his former wife or third parties. He had therefore suffered damage. Similar reasoning was applied in *Iron Trade Mutual Insurance Co* v *JK Buckenham* (1990) and *Islander Trucking* v *Hogg Robinson* (1990), which both concerned insurance brokers.

Thus in the majority of cases involving negligent advice the cause of action will accrue when the advice is acted upon by the plaintiff. However, the essential question is always the moment when the plaintiff first suffered loss. On suitable facts this might be at some other time. The point was stressed by the Court of Appeal in *Moore* v *Ferrier* and is illustrated by *UBAF Ltd* v *European American Banking Corp* (1984). The plaintiffs alleged that they had been induced to lend sums of money to two shipping companies by the defendants' negligent misstatements about the companies' creditworthiness. Proceedings were started in 1981. The issue was whether the cause of action accrued in 1974, when the loans were made, or in 1976, when the borrowers defaulted. It arose in the context of an application under RSC O 11 for leave to serve proceedings outside the jurisdiction. For that purpose the plaintiffs had to show a good arguable case. The Court of Appeal concluded that the action was not necessarily out of time. It was not certain that the plaintiffs had suffered any loss in 1974, the time of reliance on the defendants' statements, as it was not clear at that time that there would be any default by the borrowers; then it was at least a possibility that the value of the rights acquired by the plaintiffs was not less than the sums lent. That would be determined by the evidence at the trial, but meanwhile it could not be said that the plaintiffs did not have a good arguable case.

It is clear from these decisions that the question of damage in economic loss cases can be rather artificial. Nevertheless it seems reasonably safe to say that the cause of action in tort will accrue when the plaintiff's financial position is prejudiced, even though the prejudice takes the form of a contingent liability, a disadvantageous contract, a defective title of some sort or the exposure of the plaintiff to the mere possibility of future loss. It is not a question of waiting to see how things actually turn out. Finally it is worth noting that in none of the cases discussed was the later loss held to give rise to a second cause of action, and it is difficult to envisage circumstances in which an argument to that effect might succeed in an economic loss case. That would probably not often matter today as the Latent Damage Act 1986 would normally lead to a different result in cases like those mentioned.

2. The Latent Damage Act 1986

(a) The scope of the Act

Where the limitation period runs from the date of accrual of the cause of action, the claim may become statute-barred before the plaintiff knows of its existence or has any real opportunity to find out about it. This situation is quite common in negligence claims where the cause of action accrues when the plaintiff suffers damage even though it may not be discoverable when it occurs. The way in which the problem has been tackled in personal injury claims is explained in Chapters 7 and 8. In addition the Limitation Act s 32, discussed in Chapter 12, will prevent the unjust application of limitation periods where there has been fraud or deliberate concealment. Otherwise the Latent Damage Act 1986, which resulted from a report of the Law Reform Committee (Cmnd 9390, 1984), may rescue the plaintiff. This Act also addresses a second source of hardship, namely the possibility of liability in negligence an inordinate time after the breach of duty. Sections 3 to 5 are reproduced in Appendix 2. Sections 1 and 2 amend the Limitation Act 1980, and their provisions are therefore incorporated in the revised version of the 1980 Act which is contained in Appendix 1.

The Act inserts s 14A and s 14B into Limitation Act 1980. Personal injury claims are not affected but otherwise the changes apply to negligence actions generally. These must now be started within either six years of the accrual of the cause of action or three years of the date of the plaintiff's knowledge of certain matters, whichever period is the more favourable, provided that no more than fifteen years have elapsed since the defendant's negligent act or omission. In addition the Act creates a new cause of action where property changes hands while the damage to it is still latent. It also makes consequential amendments to the rules on disability and fraud and concealment.

It is clear from the report of the Law Reform Committee that the difficulties in claims in respect of damaged or defective buildings brought against those involved in the construction process were their main concern. The later developments discussed on pages 28 to 31, especially *Murphy* v *Brentwood District Council* (1990), have had the ironic result that today such claims are possible only in very limited circumstances. The Act can therefore achieve little in that particular area. Its main importance is now in respect of claims against professional advisers, though its application here depends entirely on the availability of a cause of action in negligence. Both new sections apply to an "action for damages for negligence" other than a personal injury claim, and it has been held that these words do not cover an action for breach of a contractual duty of care (*Iron Trade Mutual Insurance Co Ltd* v *J.K. Buckenham Ltd* (1990), *Société Commerciale de Réassurance* v *ERAS (International) Ltd* (1992)). Even if they did, the results in practice would be no different. In latent damage cases s 14A(2) excludes the operation of s 2, the basic six year rule in tort, but not s 5, the corresponding provision for contract claims. Any contractual cause of action is therefore barred by that section six years from the date of the breach, and there could be no room for the operation of the alternative "date of knowledge" provisions. Many professional relationships are regarded as giving rise to concurrent duties in contract and tort and in such cases the reforms will of course apply. However, recent appellate decisions have shown a lack of enthusiasm for concurrent liability; see pages 26 and 27. If it were to be held that a professional's duty to his client is purely contractual, the operation of the Latent Damage Act would be confined to instances where such a person is liable to someone who is not his client. It is clear from their report (paragraph 4.4) that the Law Reform Committee did not intend the new rules to apply to contract actions.

It is undecided whether the 1986 Act is confined to the tort of negligence. It may extend to other torts in circumstances where liability depends on carelessness. This is simply a question of construction of the expression "action for damages for negligence" used in s 14A and s 14B. The Act may also apply to a statutory liability for carelessness. The most important example is no doubt that created by the Misrepresentation Act 1967 s 2(1). The same question of construction is raised but here there is a second issue, namely whether an action under the statute is an action in tort and therefore *prima facie* within LA 1980 s 2, or an action for a sum recoverable by statute and therefore within s 9. The point is the same as that made in connection with contract actions. Section 14A(2) takes latent damage claims out of the ambit of s 2 but says nothing about s 9, and so an action for breach of a statutory duty of care will be barred six years after accrual of the cause of action if it is governed by s 9. This issue is discussed in Chapter 11 (see page 78), where it is suggested that the relevant provision is in fact s 2. If that is correct, the Latent Damage Act may apply. It would be highly anomalous if there were a difference for limitation purposes between actions under *Hedley Byrne* v *Heller* and those under the Misrepresentation Act 1967.

The case of *Bell* v *Peter Browne & Co*, already discussed (see pages 18 and 32), can be used to illustrate the effect of the 1986 Act. It will be remembered that the solicitor's negligence consisted in failing to take steps to protect a husband's interest in the matrimonial home when it was put into the wife's sole name in 1978. The Court of Appeal held that the causes of action in both contract and tort accrued in 1978 and were therefore statute-barred in 1984, three years before the issue of the writ. If the Act had been in force at the relevant time the plaintiff would no doubt have been able to say that he did not have the necessary knowledge for s 14A until 1986 when the wife sold the property and he received nothing. That would have given him the benefit of the alternative three year limitation period running from the date of his knowledge and his action, begun in 1987, would have been in time. The long-stop of s 14B would not have defeated the claim as the fifteen year period would have run from the time of the negligent omissions in 1978 and been still current at the time of the commencement of the action. The relevance of the Act depends entirely on the continued recognition of a tortious duty of care in this type of case.

There is no overlap between s 32 and ss 14A and 14B. Section 32 covers three types of case. Only one of these, namely cases where a fact relevant to the plaintiff's right of action has been deliberately concealed from him by the defendant, could have any relevance in a negligence action. By s 32(5) such cases are excluded from the ambit of ss 14A and 14B and are therefore governed by ss 2 and 32.

(b) The date of knowledge

Section 14A does not use the words "latent" or "discoverable". It applies to the exclusion of s 2 where certain facts specified in subss(6)–(8) are not within the plaintiff's knowledge, actual or constructive, when the cause of action accrues. If the facts are known at that stage it is not a latent damage case at all and s 2 will apply in the normal way. Section 14A(3) and (4) provide that the limitation period is either six years from the date when the cause of action accrues or, if it is more favourable to the plaintiff, three years from his eventual acquisition of the relevant knowledge. By s 14B both alternatives are subject to a "long-stop" period of fifteen years running from the act of negligence. The question of the accrual of the cause of action was discussed on pages 28 to 33. The Act does not alter the existing rules. The six year limitation period running from accrual of the cause of action is simply the s 2 rule repeated in the context of s 14A. It need hardly be said that ascertaining the date of accrual will sometimes be extremely difficult in latent damage cases. That will presumably not matter very often because of the alternative period of three years from the date of the plaintiff's knowledge.

By s 14A(6)–(8) the facts which must be known for the three year period to run are these:

(a) such facts as would lead "a reasonable person who had suffered such damage" to consider it serious enough to justify proceedings against a defendant who did not dispute liability and who could satisfy a judgment (s 14A(7));
(b) that the damage was at least partly attributable to the allegedly negligent act or omission (s 14A(8)(a));
(c) the defendant's identity (s 14A(8)(b));
(d) in vicarious liability cases, the identity of the person primarily liable and the additional facts supporting an action against the defendant (s 14A(8)(c)).

By subs (9) knowledge that acts or omissions did or did not as a matter of law involve negligence is irrelevant. Section 14A(10) introduces the same partly subjective test of knowledge as is applied by s 14(3) to personal injury claims. However, the test of the seriousness of the damage contained in s 14A(7) appears to be wholly objective, referring to "a reasonable person". By contrast s 14(2), relevant to personal injury claims, refers to "the person whose date of knowledge is in question", a phrase which clearly involves a degree of subjectivity. This is the only substantial difference between the two sets of provisions. In places the wording of s 14A is very similar to that found in s 14, and so decisions in personal injury claims may provide guidance to the proper construction of s 14A and vice versa.

(c) The long-stop

Section 14B(1) lays down an additional limitation period of fifteen years from the time of the last act or omission "which is alleged to constitute negligence and to which the damage in respect of which damages are claimed is alleged to be attributable (in whole or in part)". The words "which is alleged to constitute negligence" can no doubt be taken to mean "which constitutes negligence". Similarly the words "is alleged to be attributable" should presumably also be read as if they said simply "is attributable". Section 14B(2) adds that the section bars the right of action even where the damage has not occurred before the end of the fifteen years or where it has occurred but the plaintiff has not acquired the relevant knowledge.

This provision is not confined to latent damage cases but applies to all negligence actions other than personal injury claims. This is as intended by the Law Reform Committee; see para 4.11 of their report. Thus in a negligence action outside s 14A, both s 2 and s 14B apply and the plaintiff must commence proceedings within six years of the accrual of the cause of action and within fifteen years of the last breach of duty. This may be significant in a case where the damage occurs a long time after the negligent act but is then immediately apparent, for example where property damage is caused by an explosion due to a latent defect in equipment supplied by the defendant. If the plaintiff has immediate knowledge of all the relevant facts, s 14A will not apply and the limitation period will then be six years from the date of the damage under s 2 but subject to the fifteen year long-stop of s 14B. In this respect the new rules are less generous to plaintiffs than the old ones.

The long-stop runs from the date of the last causative negligent act or omission. This point in time has not previously had any significance for limitation purposes in negligence actions and existing case law will therefore provide only limited guidance in circumstances where a breach of duty could be regarded as occurring at one or more of several stages. Decisions in contract cases are likely to prove more useful since a contractual cause of action accrues at the time of the breach. They will be particularly apposite in instances where there are concurrent contractual and tortious duties, as in the cases of many relationships between professional people and their clients. For example, it is probably safe to assume that in *Bell* v *Peter Browne & Co* the contractual and tortious duties were breached simultaneously. Since the long-stop runs from the last negligent act or omission, plaintiffs will no doubt seek to assert the existence of continuing duties of care of one sort or another whenever possible, for example a duty to rectify an error or omission. In *Bell* v *Peter Browne & Co* such an argument was rejected in relation to a claim in contract and the decision will be significant for s 14B if it can be regarded as a good indication of the correct approach to this issue. If courts were prepared to accept the existence of continuing duties the protection of the long-stop would be seriously reduced. Section 14B may also give rise to disputes on issues of causation since a breach of duty having no causative effects is obviously irrelevant. It is sufficient if the damage is attributable only in part to the breach in question.

(d) Purchasers of damaged property

It was held in *Perry* v *Tendring District Council* (1984) that a cause of action accruing to the owner of a building when damage to it occurred did not pass to a subsequent purchaser in the absence of an assignment of the right of action itself. There had been *dicta* to the same effect in other cases. The difficulty of this entirely logical rule was that it applied even where the damage was still latent at the time of the sale. This was felt to be unfair and s 3 of the 1986 Act is the legislature's remedy. It gives the purchaser a right of action of his own in the circumstances described. However, developments in case law have deprived the new rules of most of their scope. No new rights are conferred by the section unless the vendor of the property himself had a cause of action for negligence in the first place, and successful claims against those involved in the construction process are now possible in very limited circumstances, as explained above; see page 28. According to Lord Keith's speech in *Murphy* v *Brentwood District Council* a property owner may have rights in negligence against certain types of defendant under *Hedley Byrne* v *Heller*. It seems that in certain circumstances such a cause of action might come within s 3 if taken literally, though it is clear from its wording that the section was intended for physical damage cases. But there is still some scope for the new rules to apply to a property damage claim. Suppose that the defendant is responsible for the installation in a building of ancillary equipment such as a central heating boiler. The work is done carelessly and the boiler causes damage to the building's structure. It was recognised in *Murphy* v *Brentwood District Council* that an action would lie here under the normal principles of *Donoghue* v *Stevenson*. If the damage does not come to light until after a sale the purchaser will no doubt have paid more than the property's true value and may be able to rely on s 3.

The effect of s 3(1) is that a purchaser of damaged property acquires a cause of action of his own at the date of purchase provided first that the vendor himself had a cause of action in respect of the negligence to which the damage was attributable and secondly that the vendor did not have knowledge at the time of the sale of the "material facts". By subs (5) these are such facts about the damage as would lead a reasonable person to consider it serious enough to justify taking proceedings against a defendant who did not dispute liability and who could satisfy a judgment. As usual, knowledge can be actual or constructive (s 3(6)). The provision applies to anyone acquiring an interest in the property except the liquidator of a company in whom the property becomes vested through a court order or someone in whom the cause of action vests by operation of law (s 3(4)). No doubt an equitable interest suffices so that a plaintiff will not be prejudiced if the damage happens to come to light between exchange of contracts and completion.

For limitation purposes a s 3 action is within s 14A as the date of knowledge falls after the time when the cause of action accrues. Section 3(1) states that the plaintiff's cause of action accrues when he acquires his interest in the property; it could scarcely accrue at any other time. However, s 3(2) provides that for the purposes of s 14A it is to be treated as accruing at the same time as the vendor's cause of action, namely the date of the damage. This is of course to prevent the six year period of s 14A(4)(a) from running afresh in the plaintiff's favour. If he purchases at a time when more than six years have gone by since the damage occurred, his action will stand or fall by reference only to the three year date of knowledge rule and the fifteen year long-stop. As already explained, s 14A and s 14B are excluded where s 32 applies. This remains the case where the cause of action is that given by s 3.

It has been pointed out (Griew (1986) 136 NLJ 1201) that s 3 seems to have given a consignee of goods a non-contractual cause of action against a carrier in respect of damage negligently caused to the goods by the carrier and occurring before the consignee obtains ownership. If so the effect is to overturn by accident the common law rule that the carrier owes no duty of care to a consignee who is not the owner of the goods (*Leigh and Sillavan Ltd* v *Aliakmon Shipping Co Ltd* (1986)).

(e) Transitional provisions

The Act came into force on 18 September 1986. If the action was at that time already statute-barred under the old law (because the damage had occurred before 18 September 1980), it remains statute-barred, even if proceedings had been started and were in progress on 18 September 1986 (s 4(1)). Causes of action accruing before that date and not then statute-barred are subject to the Act (s 4(2)). The position in relation to the action under s 3 is similar. The purchaser has no cause of action unless he acquired his interest after the Act came into force. If he obtained the property before then, he had no cause of action under the old law and the Act does not give him one (s 4(3)). Neither does it help him where the original cause of action of the vendor accrued more than six years before 18 September 1986 unless it was in fact still alive on that date through the application of LA 1980 s 32(1)(b) (deliberate concealment) (1986 Act s 4(4)).

Chapter 7

Personal injury claims

1. Introduction

This chapter deals with those claims for personal injuries and death which are governed by Limitation Act 1980 except those arising under the Consumer Protection Act 1987, which are discussed in Chapter 8. The 1980 Act does not apply at all to actions for which a period of limitation is prescribed by another enactment (s 39). The most important statutes relevant to personal injury claims in this context are those relating to international forms of transport. These are discussed briefly in Chapter 2. Where another enactment prescribes the period of limitation the effect of s 39 is to exclude the 1980 Act altogether. This goes for the provisions relating to disability and the court's discretionary powers under s 33 as well as for the limitation periods themselves.

Under Limitation Act 1939 s 2 most actions in contract and tort were subject to a limitation period of six years from the date when the cause of action accrued. Actions against public authorities had been subject to a limitation period of six months under the Public Authorities Protection Act 1893. This was extended to one year by s 21 of the 1939 Act. There were no special rules for personal injury claims until the Law Reform (Limitation of Actions) Act 1954, which introduced a limitation period of three years in such cases and removed the special protection of public authorities. The injustice of *Cartledge* v *E. Jopling & Sons Ltd*, where the House of Lords held that the plaintiffs' lack of knowledge or the means of knowledge of their condition did not affect the running of time against them, led to the passing of Limitation Act 1963. After the expiry of the basic three year period, a personal injury plaintiff could apply for leave to issue proceedings within a year of the date of his actual or constructive knowledge of certain matters central to his case. These provisions did not work well. In particular there was controversy over whether or not it was necessary for the plaintiff to know that the defendant's acts or omissions gave him a cause of action as a matter of law. This was never resolved but most of the cases were decided on the basis that such knowledge was indeed required. The Limitation Act 1975 provided an alternative starting point for the three year period, namely the date of the victim's knowledge of certain crucial facts. It also gave the court a discretion to disapply the limitation period altogether if that appeared equitable. With only minor changes the law was then consolidated in Limitation Act 1980, the present legislation.

2. The scope of section 11

The three year rule is now contained in the Limitation Act s 11. Subsection (1) is as follows:

> "This section applies to any action for damages for negligence, nuisance or breach of duty (whether the duty exists by virtue of a contract or of provision made by or under a statute or independently of any contract or any such provision) where the damages claimed by the plaintiff for the negligence, nuisance or breach of duty consist of or include damages in respect of personal injuries to the plaintiff or any other person."

By s 38(1) the expression "personal injuries" includes any disease and any impairment of a person's physical or mental condition. The reference to breach of duty does not include intentional trespass to the person. In *Stubbings* v *Webb* (1993) the House of Lords held that a claim in respect of sexual abuse and rape allegedly suffered by the plaintiff during her childhood was within s 2 rather than s 11. The limitation period is therefore a straightforward six years from the date of accrual of the cause of action, though there may of course be extension or suspension of time on the grounds of disability or fraud or concealment under s 28 and s 32; see Chapter 12. The date of knowledge provisions and the discretion to disapply the limitation period are relevant only to actions within s 11. Lord Griffiths, who gave the only speech, regarded the expression "breach of duty" in s 11(1) as implying breach of a duty of care not to cause personal injury, rather than an obligation not to infringe any legal right of another person. This seems to raise the possibility that an action for breach of a strict duty, for example under a contract or statutory regulations, is also outside s 11. That would be contrary to the present understanding. One result of the decision is that claims based on lack of consent to medical treatment and therefore made in trespass are now subject to different limitation rules from those applicable in ordinary medical negligence actions.

Since the section applies even where the damages claimed merely "include" damages in respect of personal injuries, it governs actions in which the plaintiff claims in respect of both personal injuries and property damage. If the limitation period under s 11 has or may have expired, the plaintiff can issue separate proceedings for the property damage as there are two causes of action in such circumstances (*Brunsden* v *Humphrey* (1884)).

Where the defendant's breach of duty was the cause not of the plaintiff's injuries but of some form of associated loss, the action is not within s 11. Thus a claim against a solicitor for negligence in the conduct of a personal injury action is subject to a limitation period of six years under s 5 (and presumably also s 2), as the solicitor's negligence is not the cause of the plaintiff's injuries and the claim is therefore not one for damages consisting of or including damages for personal injuries. Similarly, where brokers had failed to obtain insurance cover with the result that the plaintiff was not compensated for his injuries, his claim against them was an ordinary breach of contract action and not governed by s 11 (*Ackbar* v *CF Green & Co Ltd* (1975)). In *Howe* v *David Brown Tractors* (1991) the plaintiff was injured while using a tractor bought from the defendants by his firm. He applied to join the firm as second plaintiffs so that it could make a claim for the loss of profit which had resulted from his incapacity. He was entitled to half of the firm's profits and it was therefore held that the firm's claim fell within s 11. This is clearly correct but the judgments contain *dicta* to the effect that s 11 would also apply to a claim by an employer against the supplier of defective machinery for an indemnity in respect of liability to an injured employee. That must be regarded as very doubtful. Such a claim is in reality one for economic loss, although that loss is measured by reference to the employer's liability for the employee's injuries. The limitation period under s 11(4)(b) runs from the date of knowledge of "the person injured". This is of course the employee and not the employer. In principle the better view is that the six year limitation period of s 5 should apply. If the employee's claim is made outside that time, for example by virtue of LA 1980 s 33, the employer would still be able to rely on the Civil Liability (Contribution) Act 1978 in a claim against the supplier of the equipment; see Chapter 11, page 75.

3. Accrual of the cause of action

By s 11(4) the limitation period of three years runs from either the date when the cause of action accrued or, if later, the date of the plaintiff's knowledge of certain facts. In negligence, nuisance and breach of statutory duty the cause of action accrues at the time of physical damage to the plaintiff's person going beyond the negligible or purely minimal. In *Cartledge* v *Jopling* the House of Lords said that the causes of action had accrued at the time of the "secret onset" of the plaintiffs' pneumoconiosis. According to Lord Pearce this was the time when there was "material damage by any physical changes in the body". In an industrial disease claim this may be later than the time of the plaintiff's last exposure to the conditions which cause it (*Guidera* v *NEI Projects (India) Ltd* (1990)). It may be very difficult to establish the moment when this occurs but, in view of the alternative date of knowledge rule, that will only rarely matter. For the same reason it is presumably of academic interest only that where the claim is for breach of contract the cause of action accrues at the time of the breach of duty.

Where continuing tortious conduct causes cumulative harm a fresh cause of action accrues from day to day. This might apply, for example, where through negligence or breach of statutory duty an employer creates an unhealthy working environment over a long period of time and an employee's health deteriorates progressively as a result. Quite apart from the date of knowledge provisions, the employee would be able to sue for the damage to his health which occurred in the three years before issue of the proceedings, provided of course that the defendant's tortious conduct in that period continued to be a cause of the deterioration. It would be no defence that the situation first affected the plaintiff's health at an earlier stage. This reasoning was applied to a deafness claim in *Berry* v *Stone Manganese Marine Ltd* (1971). It seems that the onus of proof is on the defendant to show what part of the injury occurred before the limitation period. In *Clarkson* v *Modern Foundries Ltd* (1957) a pneumoconiosis claim succeeded in full because the defendant could not discharge this burden.

4. The date of knowledge

The alternative limitation period under s 11(4) runs from the date of the plaintiff's knowledge of the facts listed in s 14(1). These are first that the injury was significant, secondly that it was attributable at least in part to the conduct alleged to constitute a breach of duty, thirdly the defendant's identity and finally, where the defendant's liability is vicarious, the identity of the person primarily liable and the further facts supporting an action against the defendant. By s 14(3) knowledge can be actual or constructive. Subsection (1) concludes by providing that knowledge that as a matter of law the acts or omissions in question involved negligence, nuisance or breach of duty is not needed. Legal knowledge is therefore irrelevant and time can run even though the plaintiff does not realise that he has a cause of action, as in *Halford* v *Brookes* (1991). Gaps in a plaintiff's knowledge which are insufficient to prevent time running may nevertheless be taken into account in an application under the LA 1980 s 33, which is considered later in this chapter (page 50).

The inquiry necessary to ascertain the date of the plaintiff's knowledge of the relevant matters does not involve any attempt to strike a balance between his interests and those of the defendant. If the date of knowledge was less than three years before commencement of the action, limitation arguments will fail regardless of the degree of any prejudice caused to the defendant by the lapse of time.

(a) The facts to be known

(i) The fact that the injury in question was significant (s 14(1)(a))

By s 14(2) "an injury is significant if the person whose date of knowledge is in question would reasonably have considered it sufficiently serious to justify his instituting proceedings for damages against a defendant who did not dispute liability and was able to satisfy a judgment". The wording makes it clear that the test is not entirely objective. The approach is the same as that taken to the more general question of the plaintiff's constructive knowledge explained below; see page 46. The reasonableness test is modified in that the plaintiff's personal circumstances and at least some of his characteristics are taken into account. In *McCafferty* v *Metropolitan Police District Receiver*

(1977) Geoffrey Lane LJ formulated the test in these words: "Taking *that* plaintiff, with *that* plaintiff's intelligence, would he have been reasonable in considering the injury not sufficiently serious to justify instituting proceedings for damages?" For these purposes it is to be supposed that the defendant could meet the claim and would not dispute liability. Knowledge that the injury is serious is therefore not required, but knowledge of minor damage only will not start time running. In *Stephen* v *Riverside Health Authority* (1989) the plaintiff was given an excessive dose of radiation during a mammography. This resulted in four days of dizziness, diarrhoea and vomiting and also in erythema (reddening of the skin) and moist spots on her breasts, accompanied by anxiety about these symptoms. It was held that she would have been reasonable in considering that her condition at that stage was not sufficiently serious to justify proceedings. It was the judge's opinion that damages would have been a few hundred pounds at the most.

Time runs from the moment when the injury is sufficiently serious, assuming that this and the other relevant facts are known to the plaintiff, so that once that point has been reached subsequent knowledge of a deterioration in the condition is irrelevant (*Miller* v *London Electrical Manufacturing Co Ltd* (1976)). Where an apparently minor injury is accompanied by a risk of a serious condition, knowledge of the risk is sufficient. Thus in *Stephen* v *Riverside Health Authority* the judge said that the result would have been different if the plaintiff had known at the outset that the treatment she had received created the risk of cancer.

Where the plaintiff's motives for refraining from litigation are unrelated to his view of the seriousness of the injuries, they will not prevent time from running. In *McCafferty* v *Metropolitan Police District Receiver* the plaintiff wished to preserve good relations with his employer and to avoid jeopardising his job, which was only temporary. He was nevertheless held to have the necessary knowledge. The same result was reached in *Buck* v *English Electric Co Ltd* (1977), where the plaintiff did not at first consider it justifiable to make a claim as he was receiving a disability pension and wages from full-time employment and did not wish to "sponge". A plaintiff's motive is of course relevant under s 33.

(ii) The fact that the injury was attributable in whole or in part to the act or omission which is alleged to constitute negligence, nuisance or breach of duty (s 14(1)(b))

The paragraph does not require the plaintiff to know that his injury was caused by the defendant's acts or omissions. Causation may be one of the issues in the litigation and the mere fact that there is real doubt on the matter, so that the plaintiff could not be said to have knowledge, does not prevent time from running. The phrase used is "attributable to". It has been construed as requiring the court to ask when the plaintiff first knew that his injury was capable of being attributed to the defendant's acts or omissions (*Davis* v *Ministry of Defence* (1985),

Wilkinson v *Ancliff (BLT) Ltd* (1986)). This construction was confirmed in *Guidera* v *NEI Projects (India) Ltd* (1990) where the Court of Appeal said that it sufficed for the plaintiff to know of "a real possibility and not a fanciful one" that the injury was caused by the defendant's acts or omissions. He need only know that these were a possible cause of the injury as opposed to a probable cause.

Since the paragraph requires that the plaintiff should know that the injury was attributable to the acts or omissions alleged to constitute negligence, nuisance or breach of duty, the necessary knowledge includes awareness of what those acts or omissions actually were (*Nash* v *Eli Lilly* (1991)). Nevertheless it is not always necessary for the plaintiff to know the precise acts or omissions in question. In *Wilkinson* v *Ancliff (BLT) Ltd* it was considered sufficient that the plaintiff should have the broad knowledge that his injuries were attributable to the defendant's failure to provide safe working conditions, even though he might not be able to identify specific acts or omissions as possible causes. Similarly in *Hendy* v *Milton Keynes Health Authority* (1991), a medical negligence action, the plaintiff was held to have the requisite knowledge once she appreciated in general terms that her problems were attributable to the operation she had undergone. However the court also said that in a more complicated case the plaintiff might acquire knowledge only on receipt of an expert's report and in *Bentley* v *Bristol and Weston Health Authority* (1990) the broad knowledge that the injury was attributable to the plaintiff's operation was held insufficient. There had to be knowledge of some act or omission which affected the safety of the operation and that knowledge was acquired only when the plaintiff received an expert medical report. The same applied in *Davis* v *City & Hackney Health Authority* (1989) and *Dobbie* v *Medway Health Authority* (1992).

(iii) The identity of the defendant (s 14(1)(c))

In *Walford* v *Richards* (1976) the pleaded defence in a road accident case contained allegations of negligence on the part of a garage which had carried out repairs to the defendant's car. The plaintiff was able to bring proceedings against the garage even though more than three years had elapsed since the accident, because he had not known the identity of the garage until service of the defence. This provision has also been applied in cases where the plaintiff does not know which of a group of companies is the appropriate defendant (*Simpson* v *Norwest Holst Southern Ltd* (1980)). It will delay the running of time, if only by a few days or weeks, in a large number of cases including many road accident claims.

Although the paragraph does not say so explicitly, it requires the plaintiff to know more than the mere identity of a particular person. By analogy with s 14(1)(b), the plaintiff presumably needs to know that it is a real possibility and not a fanciful one that the acts or omissions to which the injury is attributable were committed by the person in question. Some support for this is to be found in the judgments in *Davis* v *Ministry of Defence* (1985) and *Halford* v *Brookes* (1991).

(iv) If it is alleged that the act or omission was that of a person other than the defendant, the identity of that person and the additional facts supporting the bringing of an action against the defendant (s 14(1)(d))

This covers cases of vicarious liability. It is difficult to see why the plaintiff should need to know the identity of the person primarily liable, who would normally be an employee. In employment cases the "additional facts" are no doubt those which establish the existence of the employment relationship between the defendant and the employee and that the employee's tort was committed in the course of his employment. Since the existence of these facts might be in dispute, an analogy with s 14(1)(b) again exists so that, for example, it should suffice for the plaintiff to know that it was a real possibility that the tortfeasor committed the tort in the course of his employment by the defendant.

(b) The nature of the plaintiff's knowledge

(i) Constructive knowledge

The plaintiff's knowledge may be actual or constructive. Actual knowledge is a matter of fact to be established by the evidence. Constructive knowledge is relevant because of s 14(3):

> "For the purposes of this section a person's knowledge includes knowledge which he might reasonably have been expected to acquire—
> (a) from facts observable or ascertainable by him; or
> (b) from facts ascertainable by him with the help of medical or other appropriate expert advice which it is reasonable for him to seek;
> but a person shall not be fixed under this subsection with knowledge of a fact ascertainable only with the help of expert advice so long as he has taken all reasonable steps to obtain (and, where appropriate, to act on) that advice."

The subsection seeks to establish the moment when, given all the circumstances of the case including the plaintiff's personal circumstances, it could be said that his failure to acquire the relevant knowledge was unreasonable. The test is partly subjective and partly objective. It is a question of the knowledge which *he*, the plaintiff, might reasonably have been expected to acquire from facts observable or ascertainable *by him*, with the help of expert advice which it is reasonable *for him* to seek. In *Davis* v *City & Hackney Health Authority* (1989) the plaintiff suffered from spasticity caused by an injection given to his mother before his birth. The court took account of his disabilities and the difficulties they caused him, his intelligence, his age and the resulting lack of independence from his parents (who were not in favour of legal proceedings) and also of the time he needed to settle down in fresh accommodation on leaving his parents' home about three months before his twentieth birthday. The same reasoning should apply where the plaintiff's disabilities are not the subject matter of the claim itself. Cases on the 1963 Act are to the same general effect. In *Central Asbestos Co* v *Dodd* (1973) Lord Reid said that "less is expected of a stupid or uneducated man than of a man of intelligence and wide experience" and in *Newton* v *Cammell Laird & Co* (1969) a very ill man growing weaker daily was held not to have acted unreasonably in failing to seek expert advice before his death. In *Pickles* v *National Coal Board* (1968) it was held that by referring his claim to his trade union the plaintiff, a lathe operator and former miner, had taken all action that it was reasonable for "a man in his position" to take. Such cases would today fall to be considered under s 14(3)(b). The effect of this paragraph is that the plaintiff is treated as possessing the knowledge which he might reasonably be expected to acquire from expert advice which it is reasonable for him to seek. Thus in *Guidera* v *NEI Projects (India)* (1990) the plaintiff had constructive knowledge of the attributability of his chest problems because he failed, albeit from entirely innocent motives, to give full answers to a consultant physician's questions about his exposure to asbestos.

It appears that a solicitor is not an expert for the purposes of this provision. Knowledge that as a matter of law the defendant's acts or omissions involved negligence or other breach of duty is not required under s 14(1) in any event. But a solicitor's investigations of evidence will normally be relevant to the facts that need to be known, and it might be thought therefore that a solicitor's advice on these matters is in a different category. It was assumed in *Davis* v *Ministry of Defence* that a solicitor is an expert for the purpose of the collection of evidence, but in *Fowell* v *National Coal Board* (1986) and *Halford* v *Brookes* (1991), both Court of Appeal decisions, the view was expressed *obiter* that a solicitor is not an expert at all for the purposes of s 14(3)(b); the paragraph was directed to experts in the sense in which the word is used in relation to expert witnesses. That therefore appears to be the present position though the point is not yet settled.

Knowledge obtainable through a solicitor is relevant nevertheless. According to *dicta* by the Court of Appeal in *Fowell* v *National Coal Board*, the plaintiff is fixed by the general law with knowledge that his solicitor actually obtains. In addition Parker LJ raised the possibility, without expressing any view on it, that a plaintiff is also fixed with knowledge that his solicitor ought reasonably to have acquired. He pointed out that that assumption had been made in *Simpson* v *Norwest Holst Southern Ltd* and the same is true of the decision in *Leadbitter* v *Hodge Finance Ltd* (1982). Furthermore in *Nash* v *Eli Lilly* (1991) Hidden J held that, whether or not a solicitor was an expert for these purposes, s 14(3)(a)—which refers to facts observable or ascertainable by the plaintiff himself—had the result that the plaintiff's knowledge included knowledge which he might reasonably have been expected to acquire from facts ascertainable by him with the help of a solicitor, whether his actual solicitor or one who might reasonably have been instructed. This approach goes furthest of all as it fixes the plaintiff who has delayed unreasonably in going to a solicitor with the knowledge that a reasonable solicitor would have discovered in the meanwhile. It also fixes the plaintiff who has instructed a solicitor promptly with the knowledge that the solicitor has unreasonably failed to discover. The overall result is that greater knowledge is attributed to plaintiffs than would be the case if subs (3)(b) did apply and subs (3)(a) did not, because the proviso to the subsection, discussed in the next paragraph, appears to be confined to experts.

The concluding words of s 14(3) make it clear that a plaintiff who has himself taken all reasonable steps is not prejudiced if the expert advice he receives is incorrect or incomplete, provided that the knowledge in question is ascertainable only with the help of such advice. As already mentioned, erroneous advice that the circumstances of the accident do not give rise to a cause of action is irrelevant to s 14(1). It will therefore not prevent time from running once the plaintiff has knowledge of the facts listed there (*Farmer* v *National Coal Board* (1985)). But bad advice of any sort may cause a plaintiff to discontinue his enquiries in the belief that his claim is not worth pursuing. This in turn may have the result that he fails to acquire actual knowledge of the relevant facts. Knowledge is not generally attributed to him as long as he took all reasonable steps to obtain and act on appropriate advice. His decision not to pursue his claim may be reasonable in the light of incorrect advice received. There were several decisions under the 1963 Act to this effect, for example *Central Asbestos Co Ltd* v *Dodd* (1973) (advice from works' manager), *Drinkwater* v *Joseph Lucas (Electrical) Ltd* (1970) and *Knipe* v *British Railways Board* (1972) (trade union advice) and *Howell* v *West Midlands Passenger Transport Executive* (1973) (a firm of claims assessors). For the reason mentioned in the previous paragraph it seems that the proviso to s 14(3) cannot apply to bad advice given by a solicitor. If that is correct, time may run, but if the action became statute-barred the plaintiff would of course have a negligence claim against the solicitor himself.

(ii) Beliefs and suspicions

The courts have held more than once that belief or suspicion cannot be equated with knowledge for the purposes of s 14. In *Davis* v *Ministry of Defence* the plaintiff was employed by the defendants from 1955 to 1971, and in 1969 contracted dermatitis. His writ was issued in 1981. He believed from an early stage that his medical problems were due to the working conditions of his employment by the defendants, and indeed a writ had been issued in 1973 but never served. The Court of Appeal nevertheless held that for the purposes of s 14(1)(b) the plaintiff had not known that his dermatitis was capable of being attributed to his working conditions until less than three years before commencement of the action. The various medical reports that had been obtained before then were to the opposite effect and he had accepted his lawyer's advice against pursuing the claim. The combination of the state of mind of the plaintiff and that of his expert advisers, which had to be attributed to him by s 14(3), could not be described as knowledge. The court declined to define the word "knowledge" but said that reasonable belief or suspicion was not enough. The Court of Appeal took the same approach in *Wilkinson* v *Ancliff (BLT) Ltd* (1986), and these two authorities were followed in *Stephen* v *Riverside Health Authority* (1989) mentioned above at page 44. There the plaintiff had trained as a radiographer in her teens though without qualifying. She realised at the time of her mammography that it was being conducted incompetently. She suspected that her subsequent symptoms were caused by over-exposure to radiation and felt anxiety about the risk of cancer. However she was advised by several medical experts that the dosage of radiation was too low to be the cause of her symptoms. It was not until sometime later, when an expert radiologist expressed the opposite view and called into question the reliability of the recorded level of radiation, that she acquired the necessary knowledge. The plaintiff's own experience in radiography did not categorise her "deep rooted suspicion or conviction" as knowledge in view of the united stand of the experts.

A rather different approach was taken in *Halford* v *Brookes* (1991) by Lord Donaldson MR. In his view a reasonable belief (though not suspicion) would normally suffice. It was probably only in exceptional cases where there is some "countervailing factor" that it would not. *Davis* v *Ministry of Defence* was in that category because of the expert advice the plaintiff had received. These comments were probably *obiter dicta*. They are an attempt to deal with the problem which s 14 creates by requiring knowledge of certain matters as fact even though they will often be in dispute between the parties. There may be no difficulty in the case of s 14(1)(b) since in view of the construction given to the word "attributable" the plaintiff need only know that his injuries might have been caused by the acts or omissions in question. But the other paragraphs are more difficult. As Lord Donaldson stated, "knowledge" for these purposes cannot mean "certain knowledge beyond possibility of contradiction". The eventual overall effect of decisions on s 14(1)(a)–(c) may be that time starts to run when the plaintiff knows or should know that it is a real possibility that the defendant has caused him significant injury. Alternatively the crucial moment might be when the plaintiff has good reason to believe that the defendant has caused him significant injury. That seems more favourable to plaintiffs since the belief that a thing is true appears to involve a greater degree of certainty than the knowledge that it might be true. It would however require the word "attributable" in s 14(1)(b) to be construed as if it meant "cause", and that is not the case at present.

5. Section 33 of the Limitation Act 1980

(a) The scope of the section

The Limitation Act 1980 s 33 re-enacts Limitation Act 1939 s 2D, which had been inserted by the Limitation Act 1975. It gives the court a discretion to direct that the limitation provisions for personal injury actions shall not apply if this appears equitable in view of the degree of prejudice which would be caused to the defendant by such a direction or to the plaintiff by the normal application of those provisions.

The discretion is unfettered and not confined to exceptional or hard cases (*Firman* v *Ellis* (1978), *Thompson* v *Brown* (1981), *Donovan* v *Gwentoys Ltd* (1990)). It is exercised in multi-plaintiff litigation in the same way as in other cases so that the claim of each plaintiff must be considered individually (*Nash* v *Eli Lilly* (1991)). The length of the delay does not affect the existence of the discretion, except in cases under the Consumer Protection Act 1987; see Chapter 8. The discretion does not apply in actions governed by statutes other than Limitation Act 1980; see page 6. Neither does it apply where proceedings issued in time are terminated by discontinuance, dismissal or in some other way and the plaintiff then starts a second action in respect of the same claim. In *Walkley* v *Precision Forgings Ltd* (1979) the House of Lords held that in those circumstances the prejudice to the plaintiff resulted from his or his solicitor's own action or inaction after commencement of the proceedings rather than from the application of s 11 as required by s 33. This was applied in *Player* v *Bruguiere* (1980) where the writ in the earlier action was simply not served, and in *Chappell* v *Cooper* (1980) where the first writ was served but then set aside. In *Walkley* v *Precision Forgings Ltd* it was said *obiter* that it might be proper to depart from the general rule in cases where the plaintiff is induced to discontinue the first action by a misrepresentation or other improper conduct by the defendant. Furthermore, the decision has not been applied in cases where the first action was a nullity, for example *Wilson* v *Banner Scaffolding Ltd* (1982), where the earlier proceedings were of no effect because the defendant company was in liquidation and the plaintiff had not obtained leave to sue under the Companies Act 1985 s 231. In *White* v *Glass* (1989) the Court of Appeal took this a stage further in holding that *Walkley* v *Precision Forgings Ltd* did not apply where the initial action was brought against a body (an unincorporated members' club) which was not a legal entity, even though the proceedings were not a nullity as the defect could have been remedied by amendment. It appears therefore that unless the first action is properly constituted in all respects the second action will not fall foul of *Walkley* v *Precision Forgings*. The reasoning of the decision is open to serious question. Lord Diplock considered that the balance of prejudice to the plaintiff and defendant respectively was the only matter to be taken into account under s 33. On that view a plaintiff who has suffered no prejudice at all is certain to fail. However, Lord Diplock's approach was incorrect, as he himself pointed out in *Thompson* v *Brown*; see page 53.

Other factors are also relevant under s 33, and the essential decision is whether it would be equitable to allow the action to proceed. The absence of prejudice to the plaintiff, though no doubt significant, should therefore not necessarily be fatal.

The final words of s 33(1) permit the court to direct that s 11 and s 12 "shall not apply to any specified cause of action to which the action relates". A case where the plaintiff claims in respect of both personal injuries and property damage involves two causes of action and, if more than six years had elapsed since the accident, a court might make a direction confined to the personal injury claim. To allow the property damage claim to proceed would be highly prejudicial to the defendant as it would be out of time under s 2 if made in separate proceedings.

By s 33(3) all the circumstances of the case have to be taken into account in the exercise of the discretion. While a particular factor may be decisive in one case it does not follow that it will have the same effect in the next, and a matter treated as insignificant in one context may be more influential in another. The cases on the section should therefore be approached with caution; very few raise issues of law. For the same reason an appeal against a decision under s 33 will succeed only in very limited circumstances. The Court of Appeal will not interfere provided that the judge had regard to all matters made relevant by the section, that is to say the degrees of potential prejudice to the respective parties, the factors specified in subs (3), and all other circumstances having any bearing on the issue (*Conry* v *Simpson* (1983)). It is therefore not a ground for overturning the decision that the appeal court might have exercised the discretion differently itself (*Bradley* v *Hanseatic Shipping Co Ltd* (1986)). The only guidelines given as such by the higher courts are those formulated by the Court of Appeal in *Hartley* v *Birmingham City District Council* (1992). They are relevant mainly to the question of prejudice and are mentioned below.

(b) Relevant factors

As mentioned, s 33(3) requires the court to have regard to all the circumstances of the case, but certain matters are mentioned specifically in subss (1) and (3).

(i) Prejudice (s 33(1))

In deciding whether it would be equitable to allow an action to proceed, the court must have regard "to the degree to which—

(a) the provisions of section 11 or 11A or 12 of this Act prejudice the plaintiff or any person whom he represents; and
(b) any decision of the court under this subsection would prejudice the defendant or any person whom he represents."

In *Hartley* v *Birmingham City DC* the Court of Appeal stated that in nearly all cases the potential prejudice to the defendant from the loss of the limitation defence will be balanced by the potential prejudice to the plaintiff from the normal application of the statute. The two are almost always "equal and opposite". It follows that the loss of the limitation defence as such will not be significant, and it is the effect of the delay on the defendant's ability to defend the action which is of paramount importance. This was one of the guidelines put forward by the court for the operation of s 33.

Where an unfavourable decision under s 33 would give the plaintiff a professional negligence claim against his solicitors for the same damages, this is "a highly relevant consideration", but not conclusive as the plaintiff does suffer some "minor" prejudice through having to instruct new solicitors, the inevitable delay, liability for the costs of the personal injury action and the possibility that he may have preferred to sue the tortfeasor rather than his former solicitors (*Thompson* v *Brown*). In *Donovan* v *Gwentoys* the House of Lords considered that the plaintiff there would suffer "only the slightest prejudice" in being left to her remedy against her solicitors. On the other hand, if it is doubtful whether compensation can be recovered from the solicitor it is likely that little or no weight would be attached to the possibility of such a claim (*Conry* v *Simpson* (1983)). In *Hartley* v *Birmingham City DC* it was pointed out as part of the guidelines offered that a plaintiff may be seriously prejudiced even where his solicitors' negligence is clear because, unlike the tortfeasor, they will probably know the weak points of his personal injury claim. In *Liff* v *Peasley* (1980), which concerned an application by the plaintiff to add a second defendant outside the limitation period, the Court of Appeal concluded that since the plaintiff was already pursuing an unanswerable claim against the first defendant, who would be able to satisfy the judgment either personally or through his insurers, he was not seriously prejudiced by the normal application of s 11 in favour of the proposed new party.

In *Thompson* v *Brown* Lord Diplock said that, where the plaintiff has a strong claim and the discretion is exercised in his favour, the defendant loses something which might otherwise be regarded merely as a "windfall", unless the delay has some effect on his ability to defend the action. This factor was influential in *Hartley* v *Birmingham City DC*. The writ was issued the day after expiry of the limitation period and the defendants in effect admitted liability subject only to the limitation point. The Court of Appeal regarded it as a clear case for the exercise of the discretion, notwithstanding that the plaintiff would otherwise have had a cast-iron case against her solicitors. The delay was minimal, not due to the plaintiff personally in any way but to a slip by her solicitors, and had had no effect at all on the defendants' ability to defend the case. If liability had been denied on the merits, the defendants could at least have raised the question of the effect of the delay on the cogency of the evidence, which is specifically made relevant by s 33(3). Where there is a good defence on the merits there is nevertheless prejudice to the defendant in the time, energy and money which he is obliged to expend in establishing it (*Thompson* v *Brown*).

The final guideline put forward in *Hartley* v *Birmingham City DC* was that since the possibility of a claim against his own solicitor is relevant to the question of prejudice to the plaintiff, it is also legitimate to take into account, where it is the case, that the defendant is insured and will therefore have a claim on his insurers if he is deprived of the defence of limitation. It was held in *Lye* v *Marks & Spencer* (1988) that the court could have regard to the fact that the plaintiff was legally aided and that the defendant would therefore be unlikely to recover his costs if he succeeded in defeating the claim. A large shortfall of costs was not an overriding factor but was relevant whether the plaintiff was legally aided or merely impecunious.

(ii) Other factors (s 33(3))

This subsection directs the court to have regard to all the circumstances of the case and goes on to list certain specific matters to be taken into account, namely:

(a) the length of the plaintiff's delay and the reasons for it;
(b) its effect on the cogency of the evidence;
(c) the defendant's conduct after the cause of action arose, including his response to reasonable requests by the plaintiff for information or inspection;
(d) the duration of any disability of the plaintiff arising after the accrual of his cause of action;
(e) the extent to which the plaintiff acted promptly and reasonably once he knew that he might have a cause of action;
(f) any steps taken by the plaintiff to obtain expert advice and the nature of that advice.

In *Thompson* v *Brown* Lord Diplock considered that paragraph (c) referred to the conduct of the defendant's solicitors and insurers as well as that of the defendant himself. Similarly paragraphs (e) and (f) referred to the conduct of both the plaintiff and his lawyers. Although he did not specifically say so, this must also be true of paragraph (a). Paragraphs (b) and (d) require no such elaboration.

The matters listed in the subsection tend to be interrelated in practice and will often need to be balanced against one another. Factors (a) and (b) will often be relevant also to the question of prejudice. However, the factors must be taken into account even where they are not relevant to that issue. As already mentioned, Lord Diplock stated in *Walkley* v *Precision Forgings* that the degree of prejudice to plaintiff and defendant respectively was the only matter to which the court must have regard, but in *Thompson* v *Brown* he took the opportunity to correct that error. The court had to take account also of the matters made relevant by subs (3), and the ultimate decision for the court was whether it would be equitable to allow the action to proceed. The balance of prejudice is of course a very important factor but not on its own conclusive; the court must have regard also to all the other circumstances of the case. There can be little doubt that this construction is correct. Essentially the question of prejudice concerns the future consequences of the court's decision under s 33, while the factors listed in subs (3) are mainly related to matters arising before that time. Some of them can have little or no relevance to prejudice.

In *Donovan* v *Gwentoys* the House of Lords held that the delay referred to in s 33(3)(a) and (b) and s 33(4) was delay after expiry of the limitation period, confirming a *dictum* in *Thompson* v *Brown*. However, the discretion was not fettered by the factors listed in s 33(3), which itself required the court to have regard to all the circumstances of the case. This included circumstances arising within the limitation period as well as subsequently. In concentrating exclusively on the delay after expiry of the limitation period the judge had therefore exercised the discretion incorrectly. In particular he should have taken account of the delay on the part of the plaintiff in notifying the defendants of the claim; this was "an extremely important consideration", which was "always relevant" in assessing the degree of prejudice suffered by the defendant. The defendants in *Donovan* v *Gwentoys* were in fact notified of the important details of the claim piecemeal over a period of more than two and a half years from the date of issue of the writ, and this was stressed by the House of Lords. It seems to follow that even delay between the commencement of proceedings and the s 33 application is to be taken into account, especially where the effect is to prejudice the defendant in the defence of the claim. This is perhaps implicit in s 33(3)(e) in any event.

The reasons for the plaintiff's delay will often be crucial. This factor is mentioned specifically in paragraph (a) and is relevant also to paragraph (f). Conduct of the defendant since accrual of the cause of action which contributes to the delay will be within both paragraph (a) and paragraph (c); such conduct may of course also have the effect of postponing the plaintiff's date of knowledge under s 14. Paragraph (e) specifically refers to instances where the plaintiff's delay results from ignorance of the law. Although that is not relevant to the date of knowledge, it is taken into account for the purposes of s 33 (*Brooks* v *J & P Coates (UK) Ltd* (1984), *Halford* v *Brookes* (1991)). In both these cases the plaintiffs' applications succeeded and it was stressed that their conduct was not blameworthy. In *Halford* v *Brookes* the plaintiff's main concern had originally been to secure a prosecution of the person allegedly responsible for the death of her daughter. Her solicitors advised her that her only civil remedy was a Criminal Injuries Compensation Board claim. She did not become aware of the possibility of a civil action until she consulted fresh solicitors several years later, and in those circumstances she could not be blamed for her continued ignorance of the existence of the cause of action. Where the plaintiff has worked for some time in an industry where accident claims are common, it would no doubt be difficult to persuade a judge that he was unaware of his possible rights. In *Doughty* v *North Staffordshire Health Authority* (1992) the court took account of the fact that the plaintiff had received discouraging professional advice.

In *Jones* v *G.D. Searle & Co Ltd* (1979) it was part of the plaintiff's case that her action should be allowed to proceed because it was only shortly before issue of the writ that an opinion from counsel had been obtained which led to the grant of legal aid. An interrogatory which asked the plaintiff to state in respect of each advice received before that time whether it was favourable or unfavourable to her case was held permissible by the Court of Appeal. The wording of s 33(3), particularly paragraph (f) which refers expressly to the nature of any expert advice received by the plaintiff, had the effect of overriding the privilege which normally attached to legal advice. The plaintiff could therefore be required to state in general terms the nature of the advice received in so far as it had any bearing on whether or not she had delayed unreasonably; that meant for practical purposes whether the advice was favourable or unfavourable to her case.

The reasonableness of the plaintiff's behaviour is also very important in cases where he delays after acquiring knowledge of the cause of action. Indeed s 33(3)(e) specifically requires the court to have regard to the reasonableness of the plaintiff's conduct in such a case. In *Buck* v *English Electric Co Ltd* the court felt that the plaintiff had acted reasonably within paragraph (e) where his motive for not suing was that since he was in full-time employment and also receiving a disability pension he did not consider it either worthwhile or justifiable to make a claim. Similarly in *McCafferty* v *Metropolitan Police District Receiver* it was in the plaintiff's favour that he refrained from bringing an action out of a hardy attitude to the disability and a desire to safeguard his job and maintain good relations with his employer.

Section 33(3)(b) refers to the effect of the delay on the cogency of the evidence. This has been a very important or even crucial factor in many cases, for example *Davies* v *British Insulated Callender's Cables Ltd* (1977). In *Donovan* v *Gwentoys* Lord Griffiths, who gave the leading speech, stated that the primary purpose of the limitation period was to protect a defendant from the injustice of having to face a stale claim. Lord Oliver stressed that delay is always likely to cause witnesses' memories to fade, opportunities for inspection and report to be missed and records to be lost or destroyed. The paragraph refers to the evidence of both sides, not merely that of the defendant, but it seems that whichever side's evidence is affected the result is to reduce the plaintiff's chances of success under s 33. It is obvious that where the cogency of the defendant's evidence is lessened, the defendant will suffer prejudice if the action is allowed to proceed. But in *Thompson* v *Brown* Lord Diplock said that a diminution in the cogency of the plaintiff's evidence lessens the degree of prejudice to the plaintiff if the application is rejected because such diminution reduces his chances of eventual success on the merits. It could equally be said for the same reason that prejudice to the defendant is reduced, and Lord Diplock's approach suggests that the judicial dislike of the prospect of a trial on unreliable evidence is strong. Where the evidence has not been seriously affected courts have been much more willing to exercise the discretion, sometimes after quite long delays. They did so in *Cornish v Kearley & Tonge Ltd* (1983), *Conry* v *Simpson* and *Halford* v *Brookes*. The reliability of the evidence will sometimes depend on the nature of the claim itself. In *Buck* v *English Electric Co* a delay of sixteen years did not prevent the exercise of the discretion. The plaintiff's claim was for compensation for pneumoconiosis and therefore involved consideration of the defendants' system of work rather than an isolated incident. Moreover the defendants had already dealt with a series of similar claims and were quite able to deal with another.

Section 33(3)(d) covers unsoundness of mind developing after accrual of the cause of action. Section 38(2) provides that infancy and unsoundness of mind are disabilities for the purposes of the Act. Where the plaintiff is under a disability when the cause of action accrues, s 28 in effect postpones the running of the limitation period until the disability ceases or the plaintiff dies. But it has no application in the case of a supervening disability. This can of course only be unsoundness of mind. Time therefore runs in such a case but the disability and its duration are taken into account under s 33.

6. Fatal accidents

When a person dies as a result of a breach of duty, the cause of action survives for the benefit of his estate under the Law Reform (Miscellaneous Provisions) Act 1934 s 1(1). In addition his dependents may have a cause of action of their own, primarily for the financial loss they suffer as a result of the death, under the Fatal Accidents Act 1976. If the tortfeasor is also killed, his liability similarly passes to his estate under the 1934 Act. For this purpose it makes no difference if his death occurred before that of the victim or even before the victim's injuries (1934 Act s 1(4)).

(a) Law Reform (Miscellaneous Provisions) Act 1934

The action under this statute is brought by the personal representative of the deceased. The limitation period is three years from the date of the death or the date of the personal representative's knowledge, whichever is the later (LA 1980 s 11(5)). As in the case of a living plaintiff the date of knowledge is determined under s 14, and so knowledge may again be actual or constructive. "Personal representative" is defined by s 11(6) and includes an executor who has not proved the will. If there is more than one personal representative, time runs from the date when the first to do so acquired the relevant knowledge (s 11(7)). Account is taken of all the personal representative's knowledge whenever acquired (s 11(6)).

Section 33 is applicable if proceedings are not commenced within the three year period (s 33(1)). The court has regard to the conduct of the personal representative rather than that of the deceased, and to the degree of prejudice to those represented by him rather than to the personal representative himself (s 33(1)). These are the beneficiaries and perhaps the creditors of the estate. If the deceased's claim was itself statute-barred by s 11(3) and (4) at the date of his death, the personal representative's claim will be outside s 11(5) as this applies "if the person injured dies before the expiration of the period mentioned in subs (4) above". Section 33 applies here also, but by s 33(4) and (5) the court must have regard to the conduct of the deceased as well as that of the personal representative in exercising its discretion.

(b) Fatal Accidents Act 1976

By s 2(1) and (2) proceedings under this Act are normally brought by the personal representative of the deceased but if there is no personal representative, or if proceedings are not commenced within six months of the death, the action can be brought by any or all of the dependents, as defined in s 1(3). The effect of LA 1980 s 12(2) is that the action must be started within three years of the date of the death or the date of knowledge of the dependents (rather than the personal representative). Once again, LA 1980 s 14 applies to determine the date of knowledge. Where there is more than one dependent and their dates of knowledge differ, s 12(2) is applied to each separately and the court must then direct that those whose knowledge was acquired more than three years before the action was started be excluded from the category of beneficiaries of the action (s 13(1) and (2)). But no such direction is to be made where the person in question would be able to defeat the limitation plea in its application to him individually. This would normally be through the operation of LA 1980 s 28 (disability) or s 33.

Section 33 applies where the action is commenced outside the three year period (s 12(3), s 33(1)). It is of course prejudice to the dependents rather than the personal representative which is considered (s 33(1)). By s 33(5) the conduct of the beneficiaries must be taken into account as well as that of the nominal plaintiff, whether personal representative or beneficiary. If the claim of the accident victim was itself statute-barred by s 11 at the date of his death, the Fatal Accidents Act claim is *prima facie* out of time also (s 12(1)). Again, however, s 33 applies (s 12(3)), s 33(1); and the court will have regard to the conduct of the deceased as well as that of the beneficiaries and personal representative (ss 33(4) and (5)). By s 33(6) a direction disapplying s 12(1) operates to disapply the provisions to the same effect in the Fatal Accidents Act s 1(1).

7. Transitional provisions

By LA 1980 s 40(1) and Schedule 2 paragraph 9(1), the Act cannot revive actions which were already barred by Limitation Act 1939. The provisions relating to the date of knowledge and the court's discretionary power, now contained in ss 11–14 and s 33 of the 1980 Act, were originally inserted into the 1939 Act as ss 2A–2D by Limitation Act

1975. By s 3(1) the 1975 Act applied to causes of action accruing before its commencement date as well as those accruing later. Consequently it could be argued that before the 1980 Act came into force all personal injury actions were subject to the date of knowledge rule and to the court's discretion to disapply the limitation period and were therefore not necessarily statute-barred at that stage.

The House of Lords resolved this issue in *Arnold* v *Central Electricity Generating Board* (1987), where it was held that the Limitation Act 1939 ss 2A–2D applied to personal injury actions which were subject to the three year limitation period introduced by the Law Reform (Limitation of Actions) Act 1954 and also of course to later actions, but not to earlier ones. The three year period of the 1954 Act applied where the cause of action accrued on or after 4 June 1954, or 4 June 1953 in a case where the defendant was a public authority within the Public Authorities Protection Act 1893. A cause of action accruing earlier became barred at the end of six years (or one year where the defendant was a public authority) under the 1939 Act as originally enacted. The 1975 Act did not remove the bar.

Arnold v *Central Electricity Generating Board* is a case on Limitation Act 1939 s 2A, the date of knowledge rule, but the reasoning applies equally to the discretion to disapply the limitation period and this was expressly stated by Lord Bridge, with whom the other members of the judicial committee agreed. The result is that neither the date of knowledge rule nor the court's discretion under s 33 can apply in cases of the *Arnold* sort and they are now inevitably out of time. The date of accrual of the cause of action will of course be crucial.

Chapter 8

Consumer Protection Act 1987

Part 1 of the Consumer Protection Act 1987, which came into force on 1 March 1988, imposes strict liability of a sort on manufacturers and certain others for personal injuries or property damage caused by defective products. It gives no claim for damage to the product itself or for pure economic loss. Liability extends to a person who holds himself out as the manufacturer ("an own-brander"), an importer into the European Community and, in certain circumstances, an ordinary supplier. The cause of action is in addition to any existing at common law. Most claims under the Act will no doubt be for damages for personal injuries.

1. The normal limitation periods

The 1987 Act inserts a new s 11A into Limitation Act 1980 and amends some of its other sections. Section 11A applies only to Consumer Protection Act actions but its provisions are similar to those of s 11, except in one important respect. Thus s 11A(4) lays down a basic limitation period of three years from the time when the cause of action accrues or from the date of the plaintiff's knowledge, whichever is the later. The Act is silent on the point and the cause of action must therefore accrue at the time of the personal injuries or damage in accordance with *Pirelli General Cable Works Ltd* v *Oscar Faber & Partners* (1983). The date of knowledge is defined by s 14, but in Consumer Protection Act cases it is subs (1A) which lists the facts of which the plaintiff must be aware before time will run. These correspond with those stipulated in s 14(1) for other actions, subject to two minor points. Firstly there is no equivalent of s 14(1)(d) (information relevant to vicarious liability). This was no doubt considered unnecessary in the context of the Act. Secondly the facts about the seriousness of the damage are defined wholly objectively, though s 14(3) applies in the normal way so that knowledge may be actual or constructive.

2. The ten year long-stop

The major difference between Consumer Protection Act actions and others is that by s 11A(3) all claims under the Act are subject to a second time limit of ten years from the "relevant time" as defined in s 4 of the Act. Subject to one possible exception in the case of fatal accidents mentioned below (see page 61), this long-stop operates as an absolute bar in all cases, even those of disability (s 28(7)) and fraud (s 32(4A)). Its effect is to extinguish the right of action and not merely to bar the remedy, and it does so even if at the end of the ten year period time has not begun to run and even if the right of action has not actually accrued at that stage (s 11A(3)).

The "relevant time" is defined in s 4(2) of the 1987 Act. If the defendant is a manufacturer, own-brander or importer, it is the time when he supplied the product to another. If the defendant is a supplier it is the time when the product was last supplied by a manufacturer, own-brander or importer. If there is a long period between sale of the product by the manufacturer and its acquisition by the consumer, the long-stop may operate to defeat any claim before the plaintiff has had any chance at all of taking action to enforce it, though he is not deprived of any other right of action he may have.

3. Property damage claims

All the above rules apply equally to claims under the Act in respect of damaged property. The limitation period in such cases is therefore three years rather than six. The Act caters for the situation, no doubt very rare, where property is damaged by defective goods and sold before the damage becomes discoverable. In the absence of statutory provision the only cause of action available in these circumstances would be that which accrues to the then owner at the time of the damage. The purchaser does not acquire the cause of action when he buys the goods any more than if the damage were obvious (*Perry* v *Tendring District Council* (1985)). The effect of s 5(5)–(7) is that the damage is to be treated as occurring only when a person with an interest in the property has such knowledge of the damage (including constructive knowledge) as would lead a reasonable person to consider it serious enough to justify proceedings against a defendant who could satisfy a judgment and did not dispute liability. It follows that where the damage is latent no cause of action accrues to the owner at all. Instead a cause of action accrues to the buyer when he has the necessary knowledge. This is not quite the same as the knowledge required for s 14(1A); in particular there is nothing corresponding to s 14(1A)(b) and (c). Consequently the three year date of knowledge period of s 11A(4)(b) does not necessarily run against the plaintiff merely because he has sufficient knowledge under s 5(5)–(7) of the 1987 Act to have acquired a cause of action. The ten year long-stop applies in the usual way.

4. Section 33 of the Limitation Act 1980

By subs (1) this section applies to an action under the Consumer Protection Act 1987, but its operation is modified in two respects by subs (1A) inserted by the 1987 Act. First by s 33(1A)(a) the discretion cannot be applied in such a way as to override the ten year long-stop of s 11A(3). Secondly, by s 33(1A)(b) the discretion does not apply at all where the claim is exclusively in respect of loss of or damage to property. It does apply, however, where the claim is for both property damage and personal injuries, though by virtue of the concluding words of s 33(1) it is open to the court in such a case to disapply s 11A, apart from the ten year rule, in respect of the personal injury claim only.

5. Fatal accidents

(a) Law Reform (Miscellaneous Provisions) Act 1934

Apart from the ten year long-stop, the position is substantially the same as in the case of other fatal accidents. The limitation period of three years from the death or the date of the personal representative's knowledge is laid down by s 11A(5). Section 11A(6) and (7) contain supplementary provisions identical to s 11(6) and (7). The date of knowledge is defined by s 14(1A) and (3). Section 33 applies in the usual way where the action is not started in time by the personal representative or where the deceased's own action was statute-barred at the date of his death. However, the ten year long-stop of s 11A(3) applies in all cases and is an absolute bar, overriding even s 33.

(b) Fatal Accidents Act 1976

Where the defective product causes the victim's death, an action under the Fatal Accidents Act will lie in the usual way (1987 Act s 6(1)(a)). Apart from the long-stop, the position is again virtually the same as in the case of other fatal accidents. The Limitation Act ss 12, 13 and 33 all apply, and s 14(1A) and (3) operate to define the date of knowledge. The ten year long-stop was no doubt intended to apply in all cases but it seems that an exception has inadvertently been created. The Limitation Act s 12(2), which creates the fresh limitation periods for Fatal Accidents Act claims in such a case, commences by stating that none of the time limits given in the preceding provisions of the Act are to apply to an action under the Fatal Accidents Act 1976. Since the long-stop is created by s 11A(3) it appears to have no application in such a case.

6. Transitional provisions

There are no transitional provisions as such. However, the Act applies only to products supplied by the producer before 1 March 1988, when Part 1 came into force. The earliest time for the ten year long-stop defence is therefore 1 March 1998.

Chapter 9

Land

This chapter is concerned primarily with adverse possession of land. The first section deals with the law as it applies to freeholds. Additional information relevant to lesser interests is contained in sections two, three and four; matters other than adverse possession are also discussed there at the appropriate points. Section five is concerned with actions to recover proceeds of sale of land and section six with the effect of acknowledgements and part-payments.

By Limitation Act 1980 s 38(1) any legal or equitable interest in land, including an interest in the proceeds of sale of land held on trust for sale, is within the meaning of the word "land". So are corporeal hereditaments, tithes and rentcharges but otherwise incorporeal hereditaments are not included. Easements and profits are therefore not land for the purposes of the Act.

1. General principles of adverse possession

(a) The limitation period

Limitation Act 1980 s 15(1) provides that the limitation period for an action to recover land is twelve years from the date when the right of action accrued, and that where the right first accrued to someone through whom the plaintiff claims, the period runs from the date of accrual to that other person. Thus the period does not commence afresh in favour of the purchaser of land occupied by a squatter. Provisions explaining when a person is to be treated as claiming through another are contained in s 38(5) and (6).

Section 15(6) and (7) give effect to the first schedule to the Act. Part II of that schedule modifies the provisions of s 15 in cases involving the Crown or a spiritual or eleemosynary corporation sole. The word "eleemosynary" means pertaining to alms or the giving of alms, and eleemosynary charities are therefore those concerned with the relief of poverty, sickness and other forms of distress (*Re Armitage* (1972)). It may be that eleemosynary corporations sole no longer exist. The master of a hospital was given as an example in the Real Property Limitation Act 1833 s 29. Certain office-holders in the Church of England are spiritual corporations sole. The Act of 1833 mentions an archbishop, bishop, dean, prebendary, parson and vicar. Where the Crown or a privileged corporation is plaintiff the usual limitation period for an action to recover land is thirty years (Sch 1 para 10). If the land is or was foreshore, which *prima facie* is vested in the Crown, the period is normally sixty years (para 11). Where the right of action first accrues to the Crown or a privileged corporation but the plaintiff is a successor in title, the limitation period is either twelve years from the date when the right of action accrued to someone other than the Crown or privileged corporation or the period in which the action could have been brought by the Crown or privileged corporation, whichever expires first (para 12).

(b) *Accrual of the right of action*

Part 1 of Sch 1 to the 1980 Act contains provisions for determining the date of accrual of rights of action to recover land. The rules laid down must all be read in the light of para 8(1), which provides that no right of action is to be treated as accruing until adverse possession is taken of the land; until then there is no defendant. Subject to that requirement the position is as follows:

(i) Where the plaintiff or someone through whom he claims has been dispossessed or has discontinued his possession, the right accrues on the date of the dispossession or discontinuance (para 1).

(ii) Where the plaintiff is entitled to possession under the will or intestacy of the previous owner, who was in possession at the date of his death, the right of action accrues on the date of the death (para 2). The administrator of the estate of an intestate owner acquires no title until the grant of letters of administration (*Ingall* v *Moran* (1944)). But for the purposes of actions to recover land he is treated as if the grant had been made at the time of the death (s 26). The running of time against him is therefore not suspended.

(iii) Where the plaintiff (or a predecessor) is entitled under a disposition by a person in possession and the plaintiff (or the predecessor) has not taken possession, the right of action accrues on the date of the disposition (para 3).

Paragraph 8(2) provides that where adverse possession ceases before the owner's rights are barred, the period of that possession is ignored should adverse possession be taken again later. But if the second squatter takes possession immediately so that adverse possession is uninterrupted, for example where a squatter conveys his interest to another, the two periods of possession are added together for the purposes of an action by the paper owner (*Asher* v *Whitlock* (1865)).

(c) *Adverse possession*

The essence of adverse possession is exclusive physical control with the intention to possess. Where there is a genuine dispute whether title by adverse possession has been acquired and it is settled by a binding agreement, the parties are estopped from going behind it and reopening the antecedent dispute (*Colchester Borough Council* v *Smith* (1992)).

This is merely the rule which applies to compromises generally. A squatter's possession cannot commence until that of the paper owner has ceased, since they cannot both be in possession at the same time for limitation purposes (*Powell* v *McFarlane* (1977)). Consequently time will not run until first the owner is dispossessed or discontinues his possession and secondly the squatter acquires actual possession of the land with the intention to possess.

(i) Dispossession and discontinuance

Physical dispossession is no doubt extremely rare. Any suggestion of discontinuance will normally be defeated by even comparatively trivial acts by or on behalf of the paper owner, since he has the *prima facie* right to possession (*Solling* v *Broughton* (1893)). Difficulties have arisen in cases where the paper owner appears to have abandoned the land but has plans for its future use. In several such cases the paper owner has been held not to have discontinued because in those circumstances the use made of the land by the squatter could not be regarded as inconsistent with his own enjoyment. In *Leigh* v *Jack* (1879) the defendant fenced the land in and stored goods on it but that was held insufficient as there was no inconsistency with the plaintiff's intention eventually to convert the land into a street. The same reasoning was applied in *Williams Bros Direct Supply Ltd* v *Raftery* (1958) and *Wallis's Cayton Bay Holiday Camp Ltd* v *Shell-Mex and BP Ltd* (1974). But if the squatter's acts of ownership clearly indicate a firm intention to dispossess, adverse possession can be established even where the paper owner is not affected (*Buckinghamshire County Council* v *Moran* (1989)). If there is a lack of evidence of any particular intended use for the land, the squatter's acts will more easily be regarded as amounting to adverse possession (*Treloar* v *Nute* (1977)). A squatter's occupation can be adverse even though the paper owner is not aware of it (*Rains* v *Buxton* (1880)). However, LA 1980 s 32, discussed in Chapter 12, will apply in cases of fraud or concealment.

(ii) Possession by the squatter

Where there has been physical dispossession, the squatter's own possession is likely to be obvious. If not he must show that he, and he alone, has dealt with the land as an occupying owner might have been expected to (*Powell* v *McFarlane*). Possession is a question of fact and the acts which will be regarded as sufficient will therefore vary from case to case according to the circumstances. Much will depend on the nature of the land and the uses to which it would normally be put. In *Red House Farms (Thorndon) Ltd* v *Catchpole* (1976) the squatter regularly organised shooting parties over marshy ground, and that was held sufficient because it was the only realistic use for the land. Usually much more would be required. In *Tecbild Ltd* v *Chamberlain* (1969) the adverse occupiers tethered and exercised their ponies on the land, and their children played there whenever they wished, but this was held insufficient by the Court of Appeal. Fencing the land is strong evidence of possession but not necessarily conclusive (*George Wimpey & Co Ltd* v *Sohn* (1967), *Basildon District Council* v *Manning* (1975), *Buckinghamshire County Council* v *Moran* (1989)). In *Wallis's Cayton Bay Holiday Camp* v *Shell-Mex & BP* and *Gray* v *Wykeham-Martin & Goode* (1977) the Court of Appeal developed the notion that where the paper owner had no immediate use for the land it was implied, as a matter of law, that the squatter's occupation was by his permission and therefore not adverse. LA 1980 Sch 1 para 8(4) now prevents any such implication of law to be made simply on the ground that the occupation is not inconsistent with the owner's present or future enjoyment of the land, though implied permission remains a possibility as a matter of fact where such a finding is justified. A mere written demand for possession does not cause the squatter's possession to cease and that of the paper owner to recommence, and time therefore continues to run (*Mount Carmel Investments Ltd* v *Peter Thurlow Ltd* (1988)).

(iii) Intention to possess

The occupier's possession will not be adverse unless he has the intention to exclude the world at large including the owner, though an intention to acquire title is not needed (*Powell* v *McFarlane*, *Buckinghamshire County Council* v *Moran*). Normally the occupier's intention is inferred from his actions, and this issue is therefore closely related to the question of possession itself. Convincing proof of intent will be required, and where the occupier's acts are open to more than one interpretation his case will fail unless compelling evidence of some other sort is available (*Littledale* v *Liverpool College* (1900)). In addition the intention must be made apparent to the world so that the owner, if he were present on the land, would clearly appreciate that the occupier is seeking to dispossess him (*Powell* v *McFarlane*). There can obviously be no such intention where the occupier is in possession with the owner's permission. In *R* v *Secretary of State for the Environment, ex parte Davies* (1991) statements by the occupier that she was a gypsy and led the life of a traveller weakened her assertion of the necessary intention.

(d) The effect of the statute

Once time has expired the paper owner cannot recover possession, and his title is extinguished altogether by virtue of LA 1980 s 17. Any right to damages for trespass also ceases (*Mount Carmel Investments Ltd* v *Peter Thurlow Ltd*). Since the title is extinguished it obviously cannot be transferred to the occupier (*Tichborne* v *Weir* (1892)). However, title to land is relative and normally no one will have a better claim than the occupier for he is in possession and the paper owner's title no longer exists. His possession will enable him to recover the land from any subsequent intruder. Matters will be different where he took possession from an earlier adverse possessor, since the limitation period for the latter's claim to recover possession runs only from the time of his dispossession by the new occupier (*Perry* v *Clissold* (1907)). A squatter is not a purchaser for value without notice and his title is therefore subject to all subsisting third party rights in the land whether legal or equitable (*Re Nisbett and Pott's Contract* (1906)). The position differs where the title is registered, for LA s 17 is stated to be subject to Land Registration Act 1925 s 75. The legal estate remains vested in the paper owner but by s 75(1) he is deemed to hold it in trust for the adverse possessor. By s 75(2) the possessor may apply to be registered as proprietor, and meanwhile his rights are protected as an overriding interest under s 70(1).

2. Leases and tenancies

(a) Rent

An action to recover arrears of rent or damages in respect of such arrears cannot be brought later than six years from the date when the arrears became due; neither can distress for the arrears be made after that time (LA 1980 s 19).

(b) Adverse possession against the tenant

A leasehold title is extinguished by adverse possession in the same way as a freehold. The squatter does not become directly liable on the covenants contained in the lease (*Tichborne* v *Weir*). This is because he is not an assignee of the tenant's interest and there is therefore no privity of estate between him and the landlord. However, a right of re-entry for non-performance of covenant remains enforceable and the squatter is not entitled to relief against forfeiture under Law of Property Act 1925 s 146 (*Tickner* v *Buzzacott* (1965)).

In *Fairweather* v *St. Marylebone Property Co Ltd* (1963) the paper owner surrendered the lease after a squatter had acquired title by adverse possession to part of the property, and the House of Lords held that this gave the landlord an immediate right to recover possession. The same applies where the tenant acquires the freehold reversion (*Taylor* v *Twinberrow* (1930)). Both cases concerned unregistered leaseholds. The position may be different where the lease is registered. In *Spectrum Investment Co* v *Holmes* (1981) the surrender was ineffective as the tenant had ceased to be the registered proprietor, the squatter having applied successfully under Land Registration Act 1925 s 75(2).

(c) Adverse possession against the landlord

Adverse possession against a tenant does not affect the landlord because his right of action normally accrues only when his interest falls into possession on the determination of the lease. It will accrue before then where the tenant has a written lease and pays the rent, not being less than ten pounds, to someone wrongfully claiming entitlement to the reversion. The right accrues on the date of the first such payment. This is the effect of LA 1980 Sch 1 para 6, which does not apply to leases granted by the Crown. Receipt of the rent by the person wrongfully claiming the reversion is treated as adverse possession (para 8(3)(b)). The result of any payment of rent to the landlord within the twelve year period is to stop the running of time (para 6(1)(c)).

During the lease the tenant's occupation is by consent, even where he is in breach of covenant. By LA 1980 s 38(7) a right of entry is to be treated in the same way as an action to recover land. It will cease to be exercisable twelve years after the date on which "the forfeiture was incurred or the condition broken" (para 7(1)). In this case, however, the expiry of the limitation period does not serve to extinguish the landlord's estate (para 7(2)). If the tenant does not give up possession at the determination of the lease or tenancy a right of action accrues to the landlord at that stage (para 4). But a periodic tenancy made orally is to be treated for these purposes as determining at the end of the first period of the tenancy and the landlord's right of action as accruing then or, if later, on the date of the last receipt of rent (para 5). In such a case, therefore, the tenant's failure to pay rent will eventually serve to defeat the landlord's title (*Hayward* v *Chaloner* (1968)). His right to the arrears of rent is then also extinguished (*Re Jolly* (1900)).

3. Adverse possession of settled land and land held on trust for sale

With certain modifications, LA 1980 applies to equitable interests in land or in the proceeds of sale of land held on trust in the same way as to legal estates (s 18(1)). Thus a person entitled to an equitable interest in possession will acquire a right of action in accordance with the rules set out in the first section of this chapter and the period of twelve years under s 15(1) will apply. Where the adverse possession commenced before the plaintiff's interest fell into possession, the right of action accrues only when his interest does fall into possession by the determination of the preceding interest (Sch 1 para 4). By s 15(2) the limitation period is then either twelve years from the date when the right of action accrued to the person entitled to the preceding interest or six years from the date when the plaintiff's own right of action accrued, whichever period expires later. Where the plaintiff is the Crown or a spiritual or eleemosynary corporation sole, the periods are thirty years and twelve years respectively (Sch 1 para 13). Section 15(2) does not apply to an interest expectant on the determination of an entail in possession which could have been barred by the tenant in tail (s 15(3)). The result is that s 15(1) applies and the plaintiff must sue within twelve years of the date when the original right of action accrued to the tenant in tail, since by s 38(5) the tenant in tail is treated as someone through whom he claims for the purposes of s 15(1). By s 18(3) the expiry of the limitation period against trustees of land does not operate to extinguish their legal estate until time has also run against all beneficiaries under the trust, and s 18(2) makes corresponding provision for settlements. By s 18(4) trustees or a statutory owner may bring an action to recover land on behalf of beneficiaries even after their own right of action has become barred.

If an interest is conveyed after accrual of the right of action, the limitation period for a claim by the disponee cannot be longer than that applicable to the disponor's claim (s 15(4)). By s 27 a defective disentailing assurance by a person entitled in remainder to an entailed interest can be cured in certain circumstances by twelve years' possession by any person other than the person entitled to possession under the settlement. It is then treated as effective to bar the issue in tail and the estates and interests taking effect on determination of the entailed interest. Subject to an exception contained in s 21(2), s 21(1) provides that no limitation period applies to an action by a beneficiary against a trustee to recover trust property, including land; see Chapter 10. Similarly a beneficiary in possession cannot defeat the interests of the trustees, tenant for life, statutory owner or other beneficiaries since by Sch 1 para 9 no right of action accrues for limitation purposes.

4. Mortgages

(a) Sums due to the mortgagee

By LA s 20(1) an action to recover any principal sum secured by a mortgage or other charge on property is subject to a limitation period of twelve years from the date when the right to receive the money accrued. In the case of a mortgage of a future interest this right, and also the right to foreclose, cannot accrue before the interest falls into possession (s 20(3)). Subject to certain limited exceptions under s 20(6) and (7) an action for arrears of interest or for damages in respect of arrears of interest must be started within six years from the date when the interest became due (s 20(5)). However, statute-barred arrears are recoverable by the mortgagee on redemption of the mortgage or out of the proceeds of a sale by the mortgagee (*Edmunds* v *Waugh* (1866), *Holmes* v *Cowcher* (1970)).

(b) Foreclosure and possession proceedings

Possession proceedings are subject to s 15(1) in the normal way, and the mortgagee's title will therefore be extinguished by s 17 if he does not institute proceedings within twelve years of the date when he became entitled to possession under the mortgage. Section 20(4) makes these provisions applicable to foreclosure actions also. Section 20(3), mentioned above, may be relevant to the date of accrual of the right to foreclose.

(c) Redemption actions

By LA s 16 a redemption action must be started within twelve years of the date when the mortgagee took possession of the land. Thereafter the mortgagor's title is extinguished by s 17, which mentions redemption actions specifically.

5. Proceeds of sale of land

By LA 1980 s 20(1) an action to recover proceeds of sale of land is subject to a limitation period of twelve years from the date when the right to receive the money accrued. In the case of an action for arrears of interest on that money or for damages in respect of arrears of interest the period is six years from the date when the interest became due (s 20(5)).

6. Acknowledgements and part-payments

Under ss 29 to 31 a part-payment of money due or an acknowledgement of a right often has the result that the cause of action in question is treated as accruing afresh. The general requirements for an effective payment or acknowledgement are discussed in Chapter 4. The consequences in relation to land are as follows:

(a) If someone in possession of land acknowledges the title of a person to whom a right of action to recover the land has accrued, the right is treated as accruing on the date of the acknowledgement (s 29(2)). This applies equally to a foreclosure action (s 29(1)). The acknowledgement binds all other persons in possession during the ensuing period of limitation (s 31(1)). An offer to purchase the land or to pay rent would no doubt suffice for this purpose.

(b) Where the plaintiff is a mortgagee bringing possession or foreclosure proceedings and a person in possession of the land or liable for the mortgage debt makes a payment in respect of the debt, the right of action is treated as accruing on the date of the payment (s 29(3)). Again, all others in possession are equally bound during the ensuing period of limitation (s 31(2)).

(c) When a mortgagee in possession receives a payment in respect of the mortgage debt or acknowledges the mortgagor's title or his equity of redemption, a fresh right of action to redeem the land accrues (s 29(4)).

(d) An acknowledgement or part-payment of a debt or other liquidated claim causes time to start running again (s 29(5)). This is subject to s 29(6) which provides that part-payment of rent or interest has no effect on the limitation period for claiming the balance due, but that a payment of interest is to be treated as payment of principal. This will extend the time for recovery of the principal itself.

(e) A limitation period can be extended repeatedly by further acknowledgements or payments (s 29(7)).

(f) Section 31 contains certain further rules governing the effect of acknowledgements or payments on persons other than the maker or recipient.

These provisions apply only where the original (or extended) limitation period is still current at the date of the acknowledgement or payment (s 29(7)). They therefore do not operate to revive an extinguished title.

Chapter 10

Trusts and estates

1. Trusts

Certain actions by the beneficiaries of trusts, in particular actions against the trustees, are subject to Limitation Act 1980 s 21. By s 38(1) "trust" and "trustee" have the same meaning as in Trustee Act 1925 s 68(17). Section 21 therefore extends to implied and constructive trusts and applies whether or not the trustee is a beneficiary. Section 68(17) states that "trust" does not include the duties incident to an estate conveyed by way of mortgage. However, once a mortgagee realises his security he becomes trustee of any surplus in the proceeds of sale for subsequent mortgagees and for the mortgagor (Law of Property Act 1925 s 105, *Thorne* v *Heard and Marsh* (1895)).

An agent will be a trustee for these purposes if property is entrusted to him by virtue of a fiduciary position which he occupies (*Soar* v *Ashwell* (1893)). Thus in suitable circumstances s 21 could apply to a solicitor entrusted with the management of a client's affairs or property (*Burdick* v *Garrick* (1870), *Gray* v *Bateman* (1872)). A company director is in the same position in his control of company property (*Re Sharpe* (1892), *Selangor United Rubber Estates* v *Cradock (No. 3)* (1968)). A company auditor may also be a trustee (*G.L. Baker Ltd* v *Medway Building & Supplies Ltd* (1958)). A trustee in bankruptcy and the liquidator of a company are not within the definition (*Re Cornish* (1896), *Re Windsor Steam Coal Co Ltd* (1928)).

In certain cases the beneficiary's action is not subject to any time bar under the 1980 Act, but otherwise the limitation period is six years from the date when the right of action accrues.

(a) Cases where there is no limitation period

By s 21(1) no period of limitation under the Act applies to a beneficiary's action:

(a) in respect of any fraud or fraudulent breach of trust to which the trustee was a party or privy; or
(b) to recover from the trustee trust property or its proceeds in the trustee's possession, or previously received by him and converted to his own use.

Section 21(2) creates an exception to the second of these rules. Where a trustee who is also a beneficiary distributes trust property to those whom he honestly and reasonably believes to be entitled to it, he is liable in full to a beneficiary who has not in fact received his share for only six years from the date of the breach of trust. Thereafter his liability is limited to the amount by which the share he himself took on the distribution exceeds his actual entitlement.

It is clear from the wording used that an action falling within s 21(1)(b) could only be against the trustee. It seems that the scope of s 21(1)(a) may be limited in the same way. Under Trustee Act 1888 there was no limitation period if there had been fraud by a trustee, even where the defendant was a recipient of trust property rather than the fraudulent trustee himself, but different wording was adopted in Limitation Acts 1939 and 1980. The point is undecided but it is not clear that such an action could be said to be one in respect of fraud or fraudulent breach of trust to which the trustee was a party or privy, as required by the paragraph. If the paragraph does not apply, the action will be subject to the six year limitation period discussed below.

Where the fraud is committed by the trustee's agent, the trustee is not privy to it for the purposes of s 21(1)(a) unless either there was moral complicity on his part or the agent acted within the scope of authority given by him (*Thorne* v *Heard and Marsh*). Although there is no limitation period as such when s 21(1) applies, the claim may be defeated by laches or acquiescence (s 36(2)). These doctrines are discussed in Chapter 2.

(b) The six year limitation period

Section 21(3) provides that where s 21(1) is inapplicable, an action by a beneficiary to recover trust property or in respect of any breach of trust is subject to a limitation period of six years from the date on which the right of action accrued, unless a different period is prescribed elsewhere in the Act. Different periods are of course prescribed for actions to recover land including actions by beneficiaries of trusts; see Chapter 9. Section 21(3) goes on to say that in the case of a beneficiary entitled to a future interest in the trust property the right of action does not accrue for limitation purposes until the interest falls into possession. Otherwise the right of action accrues on the date of the breach of trust rather than the date when the beneficiary suffered loss (*Re Swain* (1891), *Re Somerset* (1894)). A beneficiary's rights which are statute-barred do not become enforceable by virtue of a judgment or order obtained by another beneficiary (s 21(4)).

Section 21(3) is not confined to proceedings against trustees and may therefore apply where the defendant is another beneficiary or a stranger to the trust. It does not apply to an action by the Attorney-General to enforce a public charitable trust as this is not an action by a beneficiary (*Attorney-General* v *Cocke* (1988)). Consequently no provision of LA 1980 applies in such a case. Nor does s 21(3) appear to be relevant to claims against trustees based on breaches of the self-dealing and fair-dealing rules. In *Tito* v *Waddell (No. 2)* (1977) Megarry V.C. stated *obiter* that such breaches were not breaches of the trust itself but rather of rules arising from the disabilities to which equity subjects trustees, among others, independently of the trust. But s 21(3) applies not only to breach of trust actions but also to proceedings to recover trust property, and so a claim based on an improper purchase by a trustee of the beneficial interest of one of the beneficiaries might be thought to be within it. However, the opinion of Megarry V.C. was that an action to recover a beneficial interest in trust property and an action to recover trust property were not the same; only the latter was within the statute. His view therefore was that breaches of the self-dealing and fair-dealing rules were subject only to the equitable doctrine of laches. He added that there should be no difference for limitation purposes between an application to set a transaction aside and the alternative claim for equitable compensation.

2. Estates

(a) Actions by beneficiaries of estates

Under Trustee Act 1925 s 68(17) a personal representative is within the meaning of "trustee", and "trust" includes the duties incident to the office of a personal representative. Consequently LA 1980 s 21 is relevant to actions against personal representatives by the beneficiaries of deceased persons' estates. Section 21(1) and (2) apply without modification but, subject to a point mentioned below, s 21(3) (the six year rule) is effectively excluded altogether. This is because it is by its terms inapplicable in any case where a different period is prescribed elsewhere in the Act. Different periods are prescribed for actions to recover land (see Chapter 9) and, by s 22, for claims to personalty. Section 22, which is expressly subject to s 21(1) and (2), contains two rules. First, a claim to a share or interest in a deceased's personal estate must be brought within twelve years of the date when the right to receive the share or interest accrued (s 22(a)). If the right accrues at a time when the personal representative has become a trustee on completion of the administration of the estate, the relevant limitation period appears to be that of six years applicable to actions against trustees under s 21(3) (*Re Timmis* (1902), *Re Oliver* (1927)). Secondly an action to recover arrears of interest on a legacy or damages in respect of such arrears must be brought within six years of the date when the interest became due (s 22(b)).

Under s 22(a) time runs from the date of accrual of "the right to receive the share or interest". Administration of Estates Act 1925 s 44 allows the personal representative a year for the distribution of the estate but it seems that this does not prevent the accrual of a beneficiary's right to receive. His entitlement exists even in the absence of a means of enforcement. Time therefore normally runs from the date of the death in the case of an immediate legacy (*Hornsey Local Board* v *Monarch Investment Building Society* (1890)). If the legacy is to be paid out of a reversionary fund, time runs from the date when the reversion falls in, as until then there is no right to receive (*Earle* v *Bellingham (No. 2)* (1857)). For the same reason a claim in respect of assets falling into the estate after the date of death accrues only when the assets fall in (*Re Johnson* (1885)). Thus even a right to receive an immediate legacy will not accrue until funds are available to the personal representative. The rules on accrual in connection with acknowledgements and part-payments contained in ss 29 to 31, particularly s 29(5) and s 31(8), can apply to a claim under s 22(a). These rules are discussed in Chapter 4.

Section 22(a) is not confined to proceedings against personal representatives. It applies also to a claim by a beneficiary against a fellow beneficiary who has been overpaid or against a stranger who has been wrongly paid. But, in accordance with the wording of the paragraph, the period of twelve years runs from the date of accrual of the plaintiff's right against the personal representative to receive the property, rather than from the time of the wrongful payment (*Ministry of Health* v *Simpson* (1951)).

(b) *Other actions involving personal representatives*

The death does not affect the running of time in respect of causes of action then subsisting. This applies equally to those vested in the deceased himself and those which other persons might have against him. There is no suspension on account of the interval between the death and any grant of representation.

A personal representative is under a duty to pay the debts of the deceased with due diligence having regard to the assets in his hands properly applicable for the purpose (*Re Tankard* (1942)). A personal representative who distributes the assets to the beneficiaries without providing for debts commits a *devastavit* and becomes personally liable to the creditors. The liability is apparently tortious (*Re Hyatt* (1888), *Lacons* v *Warmoll* (1907)). LA 1980 s 2 therefore applies and the creditor must bring his action within six years of the wrongful act.

Chapter 11

Other Limitation Act cases

1. Contribution and third party proceedings

(a) *Contribution*

(i) The Civil Liability (Contribution) Act 1978

At common law a defendant had no general right to a contribution from another person who would have been liable in respect of the same damage if the plaintiff had sued him also (*Merryweather* v *Nixan* (1799)). That was changed by the Law Reform (Married Women and Tortfeasors) Act 1935 and the present rules are contained in the Civil Liability (Contribution) Act 1978, which took effect on 1 January 1979. Section 1(1) provides that "any person liable in respect of any damage suffered by another person may recover contribution from any other person liable in respect of the same damage (whether jointly with him or otherwise)". This rule applies whatever the nature of the liability in question (s 6(1)). It avails any party against whom a claim is made, not merely those who are nominally defendants, but for the sake of simplicity the term "defendant" is used here to indicate the person seeking contribution, and "plaintiff" to indicate the party making the claim in respect of which contribution is sought.

By Limitation Act 1980 s 10(1) the limitation period for a claim for contribution is two years from the date when the right to recover contribution accrues. By s 10(3) the right accrues on the date of any judgment or arbitration award, and for that purpose no account is taken of the result of an appeal in so far as it varies the amount of damages. In the case of a settlement, whether liability is admitted or not, the right accrues on the "earliest date" on which the sum to be paid is agreed (and not, for example, the date of payment) (s 10(4)). Where an action is determined by the acceptance of a payment into court, the relevant time is no doubt the date of the plaintiff's notice of acceptance. Section 10(4) has the following further results. If a single settlement involves more than one plaintiff, time does not run until agreement is reached with each of them. Where a series of settlements is made with different plaintiffs in the same action, a separate right to contribution accrues in each case.

Provided of course that the defendant was liable to the plaintiff at the time of the judgment or settlement, it is irrelevant that the limitation period applicable to the claim between them may have expired when the contribution proceedings are started (1978 Act s 1(2)). It is normally also irrelevant that the limitation period governing the claim by the plaintiff against the contributor has expired at that stage (s 1(3)). That is not unlikely given that the defendant has until two years after termination of the main action to seek a contribution. However, s 1(3) does permit the contributor to rely on the limitation period if the effect of its expiry is to extinguish the right which is the basis of the plaintiff's claim against him. Statutory time bars in English law do not normally have that effect but operate merely to bar the remedy. The exceptions are mentioned in Chapter 15. They include the ten year long-stop of the Consumer Protection Act 1987. The fifteen year long-stop applicable in negligence actions under LA 1980 s 14B bars the remedy only.

LA 1980 ss 29–31, which deal with the effect of acknowledgements and part-payments, do not apply to contribution claims (s 10(5)).

(ii) Co-sureties

A surety who pays more than his share of the debt has a common law right of contribution from his co-sureties. The right accrues when his payments exceed his share and is subject to the six year limitation period applicable to contract actions under LA 1980 s 5. In addition, an equitable right to contribution exists even in respect of payments not exceeding the surety's share. It seems that this right accrues when the surety's own liability is quantified (*Wolmershausen* v *Gullick* (1893)). The 1980 Act contains no specific provision for such a claim. However, it is thought that a period of six years would be applied and no doubt this is by analogy with the period applicable to the common law action.

(iii) Trustees

There is a right of contribution between trustees liable for breach of trust. The position is the same as in the case of co-sureties (*Robinson* v *Harkin* (1896)).

(b) Third party proceedings

There is no separate provision for third party proceedings. The limitation period applicable is that relevant to whatever claim is the subject-matter of those proceedings. This creates great difficulties for the defendant if the writ is issued at a time when his own cause of action against the third party is already statute-barred or is about to become statute-barred. Clearly this cannot happen in the case of a claim for contribution under the Civil Liability (Contribution) Act 1978 because of the rules explained above. Neither is it a possibility where the defendant's rights against the third party arise from an indemnity contract, since the right to sue on an indemnity accrues only when the loss to be indemnified has been established by judgment or settlement in the main action; this is explained in Chapter 4. In other circumstances, however, matters may be very different. As explained in Chapter 14, the retrospective effect given to most "new claims" by LA 1980 s 35 does not apply to the issue of third party proceedings (s 35(1)(a)). The following examples are taken from the Law Reform Committee's Final Report on the Limitation of Actions (1977) Cmnd 6923 para 5.5:

(i) The plaintiff, a landowner, contracts with the defendant, a builder, for the construction of a building on his land. The third party is a sub-contractor who supplies some of the building materials. Five and a half years after the building is erected the plaintiff sues the defendant for breach of the main contract because the materials supplied by the third party are inadequate. The defendant has at the most six months to issue third party proceedings (or a separate action).

(ii) The position is as in the first example except that the main contract is under seal (importing a twelve year limitation period) and the plaintiff's writ is issued ten years after completion of the building. The defendant's claim against the third party is already statute-barred.

(iii) The third party sells goods to the defendant under a contract providing that any claim by the defendant in respect of the goods must be brought within two years. The defendant resells the goods to the plaintiff under a contract which contains no such term. Four years later the plaintiff sues the defendant in respect of defects in the goods. Unless the contractual limitation period is invalid, it is too late for third party proceedings.

2. Judgments

An action on a judgment is subject to a limitation period of six years from the date when it becomes enforceable (LA 1980 s 24). Such actions are extremely rare as the plaintiff will almost always proceed by enforcement of the judgment rather than by a separate action. It was held in *Pritchett* v *English & Colonial Syndicate* (1899) that an action on a judgment could be dismissed as an abuse of process if there is a more appropriate method for the plaintiff to obtain his remedy. Proceedings for the enforcement of a judgment, as opposed to an action on the judgment, may be regulated by rules of court but are not subject to any provision of LA 1980. In particular, an application to issue execution of a judgment or to renew an existing warrant is not an "action" within s 38(1) of the Act, and so s 24 has no application (*W.T. Lamb & Sons* v *Rider* (1948), *National Westminster Bank plc* v *Powney* (1989)).

Foreign judgments are not within s 24 as they are treated in England and Wales as simple contract debts (*Williams* v *Jones* (1845), *Grant* v *Easton* (1883)). They are therefore subject to the six year period of s 5. Alternatively a foreign judgment may be enforceable under the Civil Jurisdictions and Judgments Acts 1982 and 1991.

By LA 1980 s 24(2) arrears of interest on a judgment debt may not be recovered later than six years from the date when the interest became due.

3. Specialties

The term "specialty" covers covenants and contracts under seal, judgments and statutes (*R* v *Williams* (1942), *Cork and Bandon Railway Co* v *Goode* (1853)). It is not decided whether a deed executed without a seal under the Law of Property (Miscellaneous Provisions) Act 1989 s 1 is within the meaning of the word. The Limitation Act 1980 s 8(1) lays down a limitation period of twelve years for an action on a specialty, running from the date of accrual of the cause of action. By s 8(2) this does not apply to actions for which shorter periods are prescribed elsewhere in the Act. The twelve year period therefore has no application to judgments (see above) or to claims for arrears of rent or mortgage interest (see Chapter 9). These are all subject to limitation periods of six years by s 24, s 19 and s 20 respectively. Neither does it apply to actions for sums recoverable by statute. These are governed by s 9, which also imposes a six year limitation period (see below). However, proceedings under a statute for a remedy other than money are not within s 9, and the twelve year period of s 8(1) applies. In *Collin* v *Duke of Westminster* (1985) s 8 was applied by the Court of Appeal to the right of enfranchisement given to tenants of residential property by the Leasehold Reform Act 1967.

The date of accrual of the cause of action is primarily a question of construction of the statute. In *Collin* v *Duke of Westminster* it was the date when the applicant gave notice under the 1967 Act of his wish to buy the freehold of his house.

4. Sums due under statutes

The Limitation Act 1980 s 9 provides that an action for a "sum recoverable by virtue of any enactment" other than the Civil Liability (Contribution) Act 1978 is subject to a time limit of six years from the date when the cause of action accrued. A statute is an example of a specialty, but by s 8(2) the twelve year period otherwise applicable to specialties under s 8(1) does not affect actions for which shorter periods are provided elsewhere in the Act. Neither s 8 nor s 9 has any relevance to a claim for an equitable remedy (s 36(1)). In addition many statutes create their own limitation periods (see Chapter 2); the 1980 Act then has no application at all (s 39).

The ambit of s 9 is not clear. It certainly does not apply where the statute merely modifies an existing legal duty which is in reality derived from the law of contract or tort. For example, a claim for breach of the terms implied in many contracts for the sale of goods by the Sale of Goods Act 1979 is clearly contractual and governed by s 5. It is equally clear that s 9 does apply where the statute creates a right to payment of a specified or specifiable sum of money. In *West Riding County Council* v *Huddersfield Corporation* (1957) the corresponding provision in Limitation Act 1939 governed a claim by one local authority against another for sums due by statute following the alteration of the boundary between them by ministerial order. Similarly in *Swansea City Council* v

Glass (1992) s 9 applied to a claim by a city council against a landlord under the Housing Act 1957 for reimbursement of the expense incurred by the council in putting a tenanted house into proper repair. However, there is doubt whether the provision is applicable where the statute does not in terms make a sum of money due but instead imposes a duty the breach of which will give rise to a claim for damages, for example the Misrepresentation Act 1967 and the Defective Premises Act 1972. The point seems to depend largely on the meaning of the word "sum", which appears to contemplate debt rather than damages. It has practical importance in two ways. First if s 9 does not apply, it may be that actions of this sort are claims in tort for the purposes of the 1980 Act and are therefore governed by s 2. Although both sections are to the same effect, only actions within s 2 can be subject to the generally more favourable provisions of s 14A and s 14B, which are derived from the Latent Damage Act 1986. The reasons for this are given in Chapter 6. Its main importance is no doubt in the context of liability under the Misrepresentation Act 1967 s 2(1). Secondly, if neither s 9 nor s 2 applies, the claim will be subject to a limitation period of twelve years under s 8, since a statute is an example of a specialty.

Before Limitation Act 1939 a distinction existed between an action brought on a statute and an action to enforce a cause of action given by a statute; only the former was subject to the twenty year limitation period then applicable to specialties under the Civil Procedure Act 1833 s 3 (*Gutsell* v *Reeve* (1936), *Pratt* v *Cook, Son & Co (St. Pauls) Ltd* (1939)). This distinction was essentially the same as that between such cases as *Swansea City Council* v *Glass* (action on a statute) and a claim under a statute like the Misrepresentation Act 1967 (cause of action given by a statute). In *Central Electricity Generating Board* v *Halifax Corporation* (1963) Lord Reid seemed to suggest that the distinction had been abolished by Limitation Act 1939 s 2(1)(d) which applied to "actions to recover any sum recoverable by virtue of any enactment", as LA 1980 s 9 does today. However, in *Sevcon Ltd* v *Lucas CAV Ltd* (1986) a claim under the Patents Act 1949 for infringement of patent was treated by a unanimous House of Lords as a claim in tort and therefore subject to s 2 of the 1980 Act rather than s 9. Although there was no dispute between the parties on the point and virtually no discussion of it in the speech of Lord Mackay, the decision is support for the view that it is still necessary to make the distinction and that an action under a statute is not necessarily within s 9 simply because it is a claim for money. Further support for that proposition is to be found in *UBAF Ltd* v *European American Banking Corporation* (1984), where the Court of Appeal assumed, again without argument, that a claim under Misrepresentation Act 1967 s 2(1) falls within LA 1980 s 2.

If the claim in *Sevcon Ltd* v *Lucas CAV Ltd* was not within s 9, the limitation period had to be either the twelve years of s 8 (specialties) or the six years of s 2 (tort). A twelve year limitation period would have been highly anomalous and the decision in the case avoids that result. It therefore appears that a claim for damages in respect of a statutory cause of action, including proceedings under the Misrepresentation Act 1967 s 2(1), falls within LA s 2 rather than s 9 or s 8. The same would apply to an action for breach of statutory duty where the statute creates the duty by implication rather than expressly, though most such actions are for personal injuries and are therefore governed by ss 11 to 14 in any case. An action for a remedy other than money is clearly outside s 9 and the limitation period will be the twelve years of s 8.

Where s 9 does apply, ascertainment of the date of accrual of the cause of action will be essentially a question of construction of the statute (*Yorkshire Electricity Board* v *British Telecommunications plc* (1986), *Swansea City Council* v *Glass*). Some of the statute's requirements may be categorised as merely procedural and therefore not essential to the existence of the cause of action; this point was discussed in Chapter 3. Whether s 9 applies or not, the statute may itself make it clear when the cause of action is to accrue. For example the Defective Premises Act 1972 s 1(5) specifies the time of completion of the dwelling as the crucial moment for this purpose. An application for a distress warrant in respect of arrears of rates is an "action" within LA 1980 s 38(1) and subject to the six year limitation period of s 9 (*China* v *Harrow UDC* (1954), on the corresponding provisions of LA 1939). The same applies to a petition to wind up a company for non-payment of rates (*Re Karnos Property Co Ltd* (1989)).

5. Accounts

The Limitation Act 1980 s 23 provides that an action for an account shall not be brought after the expiry of any time limit under the Act applicable to the claim which is the basis of the duty to account. However, it seems that the wording of the section is not apt to cover a claim where the duty to account is based on a fiduciary relationship and nothing more (*Attorney-General* v *Cocke* (1988)). The result is that there is then no period of limitation as such but the claim could no doubt be barred by acquiescence or laches. These are discussed in Chapter 2.

6. Arbitrations

(a) Time limits for commencement of arbitrations

The Limitation Act 1980 and any other limitation enactment whenever passed apply to arbitrations in the same way as to High Court actions (s 34(1), (6) and (7)). Effect must therefore be given to any relevant limitation defences raised by the parties. This goes for statutory arbitrations as well as those resulting from arbitration agreements (s 34(6)). In the case of a statutory arbitration any period of limitation prescribed by or under the relevant Act will apply to the exclusion of those laid down by the 1980 Act (s 39). The date of accrual of the cause of action is determined in the normal way, and a claim in an arbitration agreement providing for accrual to be delayed until an award is made (a *Scott* v *Avery* clause) is disregarded for both arbitrations and other proceedings (s 34(2)). A contractual limitation period shorter than that which would otherwise apply is valid but, except in the case of a statutory arbitration, the court can extend time for commencement under the Arbitration Act 1950 s 27, and this is so even where the arbitrator has a similar discretion under the arbitration agreement itself (*Comdel Commodities Ltd* v *Siporex Trade SA (No 2)* (1990)). By s 34(3) and (6) an arbitration is commenced for limitation purposes when one party serves the other with a notice requiring either appointment of an arbitrator or agreement on such an appointment. If the arbitrator is specified in the arbitration agreement, the relevant time is the date of service of a notice requiring submission of the dispute to him. Various methods of service are possible under s 34(4). Where the High Court orders an award to be set aside or, after an arbitration has started, that the arbitration agreement should cease to have effect, it may also order that the period between commencement of the arbitration and the order itself be excluded in calculating the limitation period for proceedings in respect of the dispute.

(b) Time limits for actions to enforce arbitration awards

Unless the arbitration agreement is under seal, an action to enforce an arbitrator's award is subject to a limitation period of six years from the date when the cause of action accrued (LA 1980 s 7). This action is founded on breach of an implied term in the arbitration agreement that the parties will comply with the arbitrator's decision (*Agromet Motoimport* v *Maulden Engineering Co (Beds) Ltd* (1985)). It is thus not an action on the award itself, but the cause of action will nevertheless accrue at the date of the defendant's failure to honour the award for this will be breach of the arbitration agreement. Section 7 does not apply where the arbitration agreement is under seal. An agreement under seal is an example of a specialty and since an action to enforce an award is one for breach of the arbitration agreement, it will be subject to a limitation period of twelve years from accrual of the cause of action under LA 1980 s 8(1). A statutory arbitration is within s 7, as it does not involve submission to arbitration by an agreement under seal, and the limitation period is therefore six years.

The Arbitration Act 1950 s 26 provides that with leave of the High Court an arbitration award may be enforced in the same way as a judgment, and this is the more usual method of enforcement. The Courts and Legal Services Act 1990 s 102 enables an arbitration claim to be dismissed for want of prosecution; see Chapter 13.

Chapter 12

Disability; fraud, concealment and mistake

1. Disability

Limitation Act 1980 ss 28 and 28A extend the limitation periods in cases of disability. Infancy and unsoundness of mind are disabilities for the purposes of the Act (s 38(2)). An infant is someone under the age of eighteen (Family Law Reform Act 1969 s 1). A person is of unsound mind if he is incapable of managing and administering his property and affairs by reason of mental disorder within the meaning of the Mental Health Act 1983 (s 38(3)). Section 38(4) adds that a person is conclusively presumed to be of unsound mind while liable to be detained or subject to guardianship under the 1983 Act or while receiving treatment as an in-patient immediately after a period when he was liable to be detained or subject to guardianship.

Section 28(1) provides that where the plaintiff is under a disability on the date when the right of action accrues, he may sue within a further period of six years from the date when the disability ceases. If he dies while under disability the action can be brought within six years of the death. The section has no application unless the disability exists on the date when the cause of action accrues. Extensions on account of supervening mental incapacity are available in some cases under s 28A, discussed below. A plaintiff's disability is irrelevant if the cause of action accrued originally to someone through whom he claims and who was not himself under a disability (s 28(2)). Similarly no second extension of time is available where a right of action passes to a person under a disability on the death of another such person to whom the right accrued originally (s 28(3)).

In actions to recover land or money charged on land the extension is subject to a long-stop of thirty years from the date when the right originally accrued (s 28(4)). In claims for contribution under the Civil Liability (Contribution) Act 1978 the length of the extension is two years (s 28(5)). In defamation cases it is three years, and the court's discretion to permit the action outside the limitation period may be exercised even after that time (s 28(4A), s 32A). In personal injury claims the period is also three years (s 28(6)). A personal injury plaintiff can of course still rely on the alternative under s 11(4) of three years from the date of his knowledge if that date falls after cessation of the disability. This is because s 28 does not displace the other provisions of the Act but gives an additional period during which an action may be brought "notwithstanding that the period of limitation has expired". A personal injury plaintiff whose mental incapacity is the result of the accident itself is under a disability "on the date" when the cause of action accrues and therefore within the section (*Kirby* v *Leather* (1965)). The provision applies in the normal way to actions by dependants of the victims of fatal accidents (Fatal Accidents Act 1976 s 12(3)). At the end of the extended period the discretion under s 33 may still be exercised (s 33(8)). In actions under the Consumer Protection Act 1987 the extension is three years but it cannot override the ten year long-stop of LA 1980 s 11A(3) (s 28(7)).

Negligence actions in respect of latent damage (damage not reasonably discoverable when it occurs) receive rather different treatment. If the plaintiff is under a disability when the cause of action accrues, s 28 applies in the normal way. Where the disability arises later (ie supervening unsoundness of mind) s 28 does not apply, as already mentioned, and the case falls within s 28A. The practical results are as follows:

(a) The plaintiff is under a disability when the cause of action accrues. The limitation period is either three years from the date of discoverability under s 14A(4)(b) subject to the fifteen year long-stop of s 14B, or six years from the cessation of the disability or death under s 28(1), whichever is the more generous.

(b) The plaintiff becomes of unsound mind after accrual of the cause of action but before the "starting date" under s 14A(5) (usually the date of the plaintiff's knowledge). The limitation period is now either three years from cessation of the disability or death (s 28A) or six years from the date when the cause of action accrued (s 14A(4)(a)), whichever is the more generous. But here both alternatives are subject to the fifteen year long-stop of s 14B.

There will no doubt be cases where the plaintiff's unsoundness of mind will be such as to prevent acquisition of knowledge for the purposes of s 14A, but s 28A is clearly drafted on the assumption that the disability will not always have that result.

There appears to be a type of case where the outcome would not be as intended by the draftsman. By subs (1)(a) s 28A operates only if the period applicable under s 14A is that of three years from the date of knowledge. But by the terms of s 14A(4) this period applies only if it would expire later than the alternative period of six years from accrual of the cause of action. It would therefore not apply if the date of knowledge fell less than three years after the date of accrual. If the plaintiff had lost mental capacity in the meanwhile he would not be able to rely on s 28A but would have only the six years of s 14A(4)(a) running from the date when the cause of action accrued.

2. Fraud, concealment and mistake

Limitation Act 1980 s 32 applies to these three situations:

(a) where the action is based on the defendant's fraud;
(b) where any fact relevant to the plaintiff's right of action has been deliberately concealed from him by the defendant;
(c) where the action is for relief from the consequences of a mistake.

The section provides that the limitation period shall not begin to run until the plaintiff has discovered the fraud, concealment or mistake or could have done so with reasonable diligence. This test is of course similar to those applicable under s 14 (personal injury claims) and s 14A (latent damage). References to the defendant include references to the defendant's agent and to any person through whom the defendant claims and the agent of any such person. The word "agent" is not used in a narrow technical sense and on suitable facts may extend to an independent contractor. In *Applegate* v *Moss* (1971) a builder was held to be the agent of an estate developer for the purposes of Limitation Act 1939 s 26, the predecessor of the present provision, with the result that the plaintiff was able to rely on the builder's acts of concealment in an action against the developer. Section 32 does not refer to agents of the plaintiff and it therefore appears to apply even where the relevant matters were discoverable to someone acting on his behalf, for example a supervisor of some sort employed by him to oversee construction work. This is supported by *Peco Arts Inc* v *Hazlitt Gallery Ltd* (1983) but there are *dicta* to the opposite effect in *William Hill Organisation* v *Sunley & Sons* (1983) and the point is perhaps not settled.

By LA s 12(3), s 32 does not apply to claims under the Fatal Accidents Act 1976. The date of knowledge provisions of s 12(2) and s 14 will normally have substantially the same effect anyway, but s 32(1)(b) is in fact more favourable to the plaintiff as it requires the concealment itself to be discoverable, not merely the facts concealed. The section does apply to other personal injury claims, though it does not override the ten year long-stop of s 11A(3) in Consumer Protection Act actions (s 32(4A)). Subsection (5) provides that in negligence actions other than personal injury claims s 14A and s 14B do not apply in cases of deliberate concealment falling within s 32(1)(b). (They could have no relevance to actions within subs (1)(a) or (1)(c) as these apply to cases of fraud and mistake rather than negligence.) The date of knowledge rule and the fifteen year long-stop of the Latent Damage Act 1986 are therefore excluded, and the plaintiff has six years (the period laid down by s 2) from the date of discoverability of the concealment.

An action is not based on fraud for the purposes of s 32 unless fraud is an essential ingredient of the cause of action, and the section therefore has no application to a claim in conversion merely because the acts of conversion in question happen to involve fraud (*Beaman* v *ARTS Ltd* (1949)). Similarly an action is not one for relief from the consequences of a mistake unless the mistake is an essential part of the cause of action (*Phillips-Higgins* v *Harper* (1954)).

Section 32(1)(b) covers deliberate concealment of facts relevant to the right of action. It does not extend to facts not actually affecting the right of action as such but which merely improved the plaintiff's chances of success (*Johnson* v *Chief Constable of Surrey* (1992)). It is particularly important with regard to claims in respect of construction defects, which are often covered up as a matter of course as the building work proceeds. It is the concealment itself rather than the facts concealed which must be discoverable before time will run. Section 32(1)(b) superseded LA 1939 s 26(b), which referred to concealment of the right of action by "fraud". In this context the word was given a broad meaning so as to denote any conduct making it "against conscience" for the defendant to rely on the lapse of time. There was not necessarily any element of moral turpitude (*Kitchen* v *RAF Association* (1958)). It sufficed that the defendant knowingly committed a wrong in such circumstances that the right of action was unlikely to be discovered for a long time. Section 26(b) also extended to conduct which was reckless in the sense that the defendant was aware that what he was doing might well be wrongful but carried on without further enquiry (*King* v *Victor Parsons & Co* (1972)). The relevant parts of s 32 employ different language but it seems that the changes were intended to bring the statutory wording into line with the case law. Thus s 32(2) provides that deliberate commission of a breach of duty in circumstances in which it is unlikely to be discovered for some time amounts to deliberate concealment of the facts involved in that breach of duty for the purposes of s 32(1)(b). In *Westlake* v *Bracknell DC* (1987) it was held that this extended to reckless conduct, though that is not entirely clear from the wording. It obviously does not cover mere negligence where the defendant does not realise that he has committed a wrong (*William Hill Organisation* v *Sunley & Sons*). If he realises the situation but then proceeds without rectifying it, that failure might itself be a separate breach of duty so that the section would apply. If it were not, there is presumably no "deliberate commission" of a wrong as required by subs (2), though a deliberate failure to inform the plaintiff of the position will no doubt itself suffice where there is a fiduciary relationship between the parties (*UBAF Ltd* v *European American Banking Corp* (1984)).

Where s 32 applies, its effect is that "the period of limitation shall not begin to run" until the date of discoverability. It seems clear therefore that it has no relevance where facts are concealed by the defendant after accrual of the cause of action, as by then time is already running (*Tito* v *Waddell (No. 2)* (1977)). *Westlake* v *Bracknell DC* is to the contrary but must be regarded as wrongly decided on the point. The plaintiff might nevertheless succeed. First, the circumstances of the concealment may give rise to a separate cause of action, for example in the tort of deceit. Secondly, statements by a defendant tending to conceal the existence of a cause of action have occasionally been held to create an estoppel preventing him from relying on the defence of limitation. That was so in *Kaliszewska* v *John Clague & Partners* (1984) and *Westlake* v *Bracknell DC*—see Chapter 3. And thirdly the plaintiff in a negligence action may be rescued by LA 1980 s 14A if his date of knowledge is affected by the defendant's acts of concealment.

References to the defendant in s 32(1) include references to any person through whom he claims and the agent of any such person. Section 38(5) and (6) explain when a person is to be treated as claiming through another. Section 32 can therefore apply, for example, where property is obtained from the plaintiff by fraud and passed on to the defendant by the culprit. But where the property has been bought for valuable consideration by an innocent third party as defined in s 32(4) after the fraud, concealment or mistake, an action against him or someone claiming through him to recover the property or its value or to enforce a charge against the property or set aside a transaction affecting it cannot succeed if it could not do so without the section (s 32(3)).

Chapter 13

Want of prosecution

1. The basic principles

The Rules of the Supreme Court contain several provisions empowering the court to dismiss actions for default on the part of the plaintiff. These include RSC O 19 r 1 (delay in serving a statement of claim), O 24 r 16(1) (discovery), O 25 r 1(4) (summons for directions), O 28 r 10(1) (originating summons procedure) and O 34 r 2(2) (setting down). But in any event the court has a general power to dismiss for want of prosecution under its inherent jurisdiction and it seems to make little or no difference whether the particular circumstances fall within one of these rules or not (*Costellow* v *Somerset County Council* (1993)). The governing principles were established by the Court of Appeal in *Allen* v *Sir Alfred McAlpine & Sons Ltd* (1968) and approved by the House of Lords in *Birkett* v *James* (1978) and *Department of Transport* v *Chris Smaller (Transport) Ltd* (1989). They are that the power should be exercised only where the default has been intentional and contumelious or where there has been inordinate and inexcusable delay which gives rise to a substantial risk that a fair trial will not be possible or to the likelihood of serious prejudice to the defendant. The examples of contumelious conduct given in *Birkett* v *James* were disobedience to a peremptory order (usually an "unless" order) or behaviour amounting to an abuse of the process of the court. In cases where the defendant relies solely on inexcusable delay, he need give no prior warning before applying for the action to be dismissed.

The power is discretionary and the grounds for reversal of a decision on appeal are therefore narrow. The Court of Appeal may overturn the decision where the judge has erred in principle by giving weight to something which he should not have taken into account or by failing to give weight to something which he should have taken into account. It may also do so in order to promote consistency among the judges where there appear to be two schools of opinion on the relative importance of particular factors (*Ward* v *James* (1966), *Birkett* v *James*). The Court of Appeal will therefore not substitute its own decision for that of the judge merely because its members would have exercised the discretion differently (*Eagil Trust Co Ltd* v *Pigott-Brown* (1985)).

2. Where the limitation period has not expired

(a) Birkett v James

Where the plaintiff's conduct has been contumelious, it is not relevant that the limitation period is still current. A second action on the same facts can itself be struck out under RSC O 18 r 19(1) as an abuse of the process of the court. There were *dicta* to that effect by Lord Diplock and Lord Keith in *Tolley* v *Morris* (1979) and although Lord Salmon and Lord Edmund-Davies had taken the opposite view in *Birkett* v *James*, doubts on the point seem to have been removed by *Janov* v *Morris* (1981). There the first action had been dismissed for the plaintiff's failure to comply with a peremptory order, and the Court of Appeal struck out the second action as an abuse even though the limitation period had not expired. This is not an inevitable result in such a case since the matter is discretionary and in suitable circumstances the plaintiff may be able to persuade the court that the failure was not contumelious and that the second action should be allowed to proceed (*Re Jokai Tea Holdings* (1989), *Grand Metropolitan Nominee (No 2) Co Ltd* v *Evans* (1993)).

Cases where the defendant relies exclusively on the plaintiff's delays are on a different footing. In *Birkett* v *James* the House of Lords stated that in such instances there is no discretion to dismiss a second action for the same relief on the ground that the first action was itself struck out for want of prosecution. Consequently the dismissal of the first action would not benefit the defendant in a case where the plaintiff was likely to issue a fresh writ. On the contrary it would merely add to the costs and prolong matters still further, making a fair trial even less likely. It followed that in the exercise of the court's discretion the fact that the limitation period was still current must always be a matter of great weight and generally a conclusive reason on its own against dismissal of the proceedings if the likely consequence would be a second action on the same facts. In *Bailey* v *Bailey* (1983) the Court of Appeal specifically held that the commencement of the later action did not constitute an abuse of the process of the court. However, it appears that the plaintiff can be prevented from prosecuting the second action until he has discharged his liability for costs, if any, in relation to the first (*Thames Investment & Securities plc* v *Benjamin* (1984), *Hicks* v *Newman* (1989), *Barclays Bank plc* v *Miller* (1990)). Presumably this would be achieved by staying the second action until the costs were paid. In *Halls* v *O'Dell* (1991) the Court of Appeal held that the same principles apply under RSC O 28 r 10 in proceedings commenced by originating summons as in actions started by writ, and in *Joyce* v *Joyce* (1978) a similar approach was taken where the second action was a claim for equitable relief and subject only to the equitable doctrine of laches.

Where the plaintiff is under a disability he has until the end of a period of three years following the cessation of the disability in which to commence a personal injury action, and six years in most other cases (LA 1980 s 28). The result is that an application to dismiss for want of prosecution before the expiry of the extended period is certain to fail unless there are exceptional circumstances. The reasoning of *Birkett* v *James* was applied by the House of Lords in *Tolley* v *Morris* to an action by an infant and by the Court of Appeal in *Turner* v *W.H. Malcolm Ltd* (1992) to an action by a plaintiff of unsound mind. In the latter type of case the disability may of course be permanent. The solution suggested in *Tolley* v *Morris* was that the defendant should seek a peremptory order. Continued default by the plaintiff would result in dismissal of the proceedings regardless of the limitation position and, as already mentioned, a second action by the plaintiff could itself be struck out as an abuse of the process of the court. That will of course have to be the defendant's normal approach in any case where the limitation period is still current.

(b) Exceptions

In *Birkett* v *James* the House of Lords stated that there may be exceptional cases where it would be proper to stay a second action because the plaintiff's conduct in the earlier proceedings had induced the defendant to do something which would create difficulties for the presentation of the defence. Where that is so, it will of course make a striking out possible in respect of the first action. *Spring Grove Services Ltd* v *Deane* (1972), where the Court of Appeal had struck out a second action within the limitation period, was given as a possible example. The House of Lords was prepared to accept the result, if not the reasoning, because in the first action the plaintiff's solicitor had told the defendant that the action had been abandoned and as a consequence the defendant had lost touch with an important witness.

No other exceptions were put forward in *Birkett* v *James* but subsequent case law shows that it does not establish an immutable rule. In *Barclays Bank* v *Miller* the Court of Appeal held that where it was open to serious doubt whether the limitation period had expired the appropriate course was to dismiss the action; the plaintiff could institute fresh proceedings if so minded. Normally the court would seek to resolve any such doubt on the hearing of the summons, but the case involved a total of four causes of action and quite a substantial enquiry would have been necessary both as to the causes of action themselves and in relation to their respective dates of accrual. It was also in issue whether they had all been sufficiently pleaded. The Court of Appeal felt it inappropriate for long and elaborate arguments on such matters to be dealt with on the hearing of an interlocutory application when, if the application were dismissed for want of prosecution, they might never arise at all (since the plaintiff would not necessarily relitigate) and, if they did, they could perhaps be considered more conveniently by a different procedure. The case was cited in *Rath* v *CS Lawrence & Partners* (1991), where the same approach was again taken by the Court of Appeal.

In *Barclays Bank* v *Miller* Staughton LJ, with whom the other judges agreed, drew support from two first instance decisions. In *Hicks* v

Newman Hoffman J struck out an action for want of prosecution where the assertion that the limitation period had not expired (or that there was no applicable period) was based solely on the hope that something would turn up on discovery. In addition he pointed out that the basis of the reasoning in *Birkett* v *James* was the absence of any advantage to the defendant from dismissal of the action within the limitation period but that in the case before him real advantages would in fact accrue to the defendants. These included the rule that the plaintiff could not litigate a second time on the same facts without paying the costs of the earlier action. In *Wright* v *Morris* (1988), a passing off action in which the plaintiffs sought an injunction and an account of profits, Millett J also felt free to dismiss the proceedings even though the limitation period was still current. The litigation was primarily concerned with regulation of the future conduct of the parties and in such cases it was seldom true, in the judge's view, that dismissal of the action could only work to the defendant's disadvantage. Much had happened since the issue of the writ, and the action was no longer a suitable vehicle for resolving the dispute. The institution of fresh proceedings would permit the parties to present their claims and counterclaims in the light of the new circumstances. Moreover the judge was "not prepared to assume" that the plaintiffs would be able to obtain legal aid for a second action as easily as they might for the continuance of existing proceedings. In *Birkett* v *James* the House of Lords regarded the non-expiry of the limitation period as generally conclusive of the issue in cases where it was likely that the plaintiff would commence a fresh action if the proceedings were dismissed. Where that is not likely a different approach can legitimately be taken, though the limitation point would remain "a matter of great weight" (Lord Diplock in *Birkett* v *James*). This may justify a judge in taking account of the legal aid position and of the costs rule mentioned by Hoffman J, since they are both relevant to the likelihood of a second action. The fact remains, however, that since *Birkett* v *James* few cases have been struck out for want of prosecution before the end of the limitation period.

3. Where the limitation period has expired

Once the limitation period has expired, an application to dismiss for want of prosecution obviously has a much better chance of success. The matter is not entirely straightforward and the limitation period remains relevant in certain ways.

(a) The stage when the delay occurs

Delay may occur before the issue of the writ, after issue but within the limitation period, and after expiry of the period. In *William C Parker Ltd* v *FJ Ham & Son Ltd* (1972) the Court of Appeal held that delay before the issue of the writ could not alone be a ground for dismissing the action; the effect would be to create a second limitation period shorter than that laid down by Parliament. However, delay before issue could be relevant to the decision whether any later delay was to be regarded as inordinate and inexcusable. If it were, dismissal would be possible but only if the later delay had added to the prejudice to the plaintiff. For a time there was some doubt about the necessity for this further prejudice but the House of Lords confirmed the principles of *Parker* v *Ham* in *Birkett* v *James* and applied them in *Department of Transport* v *Smaller*. Thus delay by a plaintiff who has made a late start is for that reason more likely to be considered inexcusable. The additional prejudice caused by the delay need not be great but must be more than minimal. Where the defendant's position is so hopelessly prejudiced by the delay before commencement of the case that any later delay cannot be said to make matters worse, an application to dismiss seems to be pointless. *Electricity Supply Nominees Ltd* v *Longstaff & Shaw Ltd* (1986), an unreported decision of the Court of Appeal discussed in *Department of Transport* v *Smaller*, is an example of this sort of situation. The House of Lords was not swayed by the argument that prejudice from the post-issue delay should not be necessary.

In *Rath* v *CS Lawrence & Partners* and in *Trill* v *Sacher* (1993) the Court of Appeal held that delay occurring after issue of the writ but before expiry of the limitation period is to be taken into account, even though the time elapsed would have been disregarded (except to the extent mentioned) if the plaintiff had simply delayed commencement of the proceedings. The obligation to prosecute the claim with due diligence arises when the action is started, whenever that might be. Obviously an application to strike out is very unlikely to succeed until the limitation period expires but the defendant does not necessarily have to show further prejudicial delay after that time.

It goes without saying that delay after expiry of the limitation period is taken into account, but two points need to be made in connection with personal injury claims. First it could be argued that a personal injury claim should not be dismissed even outside the three year period of LA 1980 s 11 as a second action might be permitted by virtue of s 33. That argument cannot succeed because *Walkley* v *Precision Forgings Ltd* (1979), discussed in Chapter 7, establishes that no such second action is in fact possible at all unless there are exceptional circumstances of a type not relevant for present purposes. The discretion of s 33 can therefore be disregarded. Secondly, delay between the expiry of the primary period and the time of a successful application under s 33 is presumably relevant to the same extent as pre-writ delays in a case started within the primary period. The question of the plaintiff's delay will be the central issue under s 33, and if the plaintiff succeeds it is inconceivable that the defendant could then have the action dismissed for want of prosecution without further prejudicial delay on the plaintiff's part. In other words the principles of *Parker* v *Ham* ought to apply, and that is supported by the decision of the Court of Appeal in *Biss* v *Lambeth, Southwark and Lewisham Area Health Authority* (1978).

(b) "Inordinate and inexcusable"

Such delay as is permitted by the rules of court is not to be regarded as inexcusable for the purposes of want of prosecution. *Dicta* to the opposite effect in *Thorpe* v *Alexander Forklift Trucks Ltd* (1975) were disapproved in *Birkett* v *James*. Beyond that the matter is at the discretion of the judge, and the importance of any particular factor may vary according to the circumstances. In *Thorpe* v *Alexander* the Court of Appeal was not prepared to accept the excuse that papers had been with counsel for about four months; the solicitors should have "demanded expedition of him" or instructed someone else. And in *Rath* v *Lawrence* no allowance was made for difficulties caused by the institution of divorce proceedings between the plaintiffs. But in *Birkett* v *James* Lord Salmon considered that there was justification for the delays involved in an application for legal aid, including an appeal against an initial refusal, and in the obtaining of the documents in the action from the plaintiff's first solicitors, which had necessitated a court order. It would be dangerous to suggest any particular period of inexcusable delay as the minimum likely to be regarded as inordinate. For one thing it will differ according to the length of any delay before issue of the writ. In *Biss* v *Lambeth, Southwark and Lewisham Area Health Authority* the period of delay was nine months, and in *Sweeney* v *Sir Robert McAlpine & Sons Ltd* (1974) only six months. The actions were struck out but in both cases there had been very substantial pre-writ delays. Where the writ is issued reasonably promptly, a plaintiff might hope for somewhat greater indulgence.

(c) The effect of the delay

The delay must give rise to a substantial risk that a fair trial will not be possible or to the likelihood of serious prejudice to the defendant. Delay often reduces the cogency of evidence, for example through the loss or destruction of records. The recollection of witnesses is particularly likely to be adversely affected. Worse still, the witnesses may cease to be available at all.

In *Department of Transport* v *Smaller* the submission that prejudice to the defendant is confined to disadvantage in the conduct of the litigation was rejected. The House of Lords declined to define or categorise the type of prejudice which will suffice, but considered that in the case before it a judge would have been entitled to strike out the action if the defendants had been able to establish significant damage to their business interests resulting from the delay after issue of the writ. Commercial prejudice was also relied on by Millett J in *Wright* v *Morris* and by the Court of Appeal in two medical negligence actions. In *Antcliffe* v *Gloucester Health Authority* (1992), it was considered that there had been sufficient prejudice where a change in the insurance arrangements of health authorities had had the result that any damages recovered by the plaintiff if the action had proceeded would have had to be paid by the defendants themselves. But for the delays the action would have been tried while the old arrangements were still in force, and the damages would then have been payable by the medical defence organisation of one of the surgeons. This factor was also accepted as prejudice in *Gascoigne* v *Haringey Health Authority* (1992), although there the court felt that it should not be regarded as sufficient on its own. In *Newman* v *Hopkins* (1988) the appeal court stated that account could be taken of an increase in the defendant's liability for damages which resulted from the delay. But in *Turner* v *WH Malcolm Ltd* Staughton LJ pointed out that in the case before him it could be argued that the financial prejudice caused to the defendants through the need to revise the plaintiff's life expectancy arose merely because the original estimate had been wrong. Moreover, it could be argued that the increased liability for interest on the damages was not seriously prejudicial as the defendants or their insurers had had the use of the money in the meanwhile and the plaintiff had not.

The anxiety which the pending action causes to a defendant, or perhaps to those for whom he is vicariously liable, may also amount to prejudice (*Biss* v *Lambeth, Southwark and Lewisham Area Health Authority*, *Gascoigne* v *Haringey Health Authority*). However, in *Department of Transport* v *Smaller* Lord Griffiths stated that such anxiety would be sufficient on its own only in exceptional cases. *Biss* v *Lambeth AHA* was in that category as the action had been in progress for eleven and a half years and professional reputations were at stake.

The plaintiff's culpable delay must have been the cause of the prejudice. *Department of Transport* v *Smaller* shows that it will not avail the defendant if the prejudice would have existed even if the claim had been pursued diligently after the issue of the writ. The effect of the delay must be judged by comparing the situation at the time of the striking-out application with the position as it would probably have been if the action had proceeded at a proper pace. It seems that only prejudice to the defendant is relevant and that there is therefore no question of balancing the prejudice to the defendant against the prejudice that the plaintiff will suffer if the action is dismissed (*Pattison* v *Hobbs* (1985)). There are statements to the opposite effect by Wolfe LJ in *Gascoigne* v *Haringey Health Authority* but no support for his approach is to be found in *Birkett* v *James* or *Department of Transport* v *Smaller*. In particular the speeches in *Birkett* v *James*, Salmon LJ dissenting on the point, make it clear that the plaintiff's prospects of success in a negligence action against his own solicitor after a striking out are irrelevant.

(d) The conduct of the defendant

Plainly the defendant cannot rely on delays for which he was responsible himself and in addition the court is entitled to take account of these delays, and indeed of the defendant's conduct generally, in the exercise of its discretion. Contribution to the delay by the defendants was an influential factor in *Instrumatic Ltd* v *Supabrase Ltd* (1969) and *Austin Securities Ltd* v *Northgate & English Stores Ltd* (1969).

There is a serious danger that the defendant will prejudice his chances if he does not apply to strike out promptly once the action comes back to life. It now appears established that the application will fail where the defendant has conducted himself in such a way as to induce the plaintiff to incur further costs, not being merely minimal or negligible, in the reasonable belief that he intends to allow the case to proceed to trial in spite of the delays. Such conduct appears to give rise to a form of estoppel. Passive inaction by the defendant will not suffice for this purpose and in particular he is under no obligation to make the striking-out application within the one month period following service by the plaintiff of a notice of intention to proceed under RSC O 3 r 6 (*Trill* v *Sacher* (1993)). But positive action will remove any justification for an application to dismiss unless it is followed by further culpable delay on the plaintiff's part. Statements to this effect were made by both Diplock LJ and Salmon LJ in *Allen* v *McAlpine*. In *County & District Properties Ltd* v *Lyell*, decided in 1977 but unreported until 1991, the Court of Appeal held in accordance with those *dicta* that such action by the defendant was not simply a factor to be taken into account in the exercise of the discretion; it removed the discretion altogether. That decision was followed by the Court of Appeal in *Reynolds* v *British Leyland Ltd* (1991), *Armstrong* v *Glofield Properties Ltd* (1992) and *Roche* v *Church* (1992), where it was further held that it is not open to the defendant to defeat the estoppel by offering to compensate the plaintiff for the costs incurred in this way.

However, it did not affect the result in all the cases mentioned. In *County & District Properties* v *Lyell* the plaintiffs' solicitors served notice of intention to proceed followed at roughly monthly intervals by long-outstanding further and better particulars of the statement of claim and a summons for directions. The defendant's solicitors acknowledged receipt on each occasion. Both sides attended the hearing of the summons some twelve weeks later and a consent order was made transferring the action to an official referee. When the summons came on before him after a further fortnight it was adjourned again, and three weeks later the summons to dismiss for want of prosecution was issued. It was held that the positive actions on the defendant's side precluded him from obtaining a striking-out order. The plaintiffs should be allowed to continue the action however difficult their "shocking" delay had made it for the court to do justice. It was the defendant's solicitor's attendance at the two hearings and his agreement to the order made at the first which counted most against him. He certainly seemed to be acting as if the action would continue to trial, and the idea of an application to dismiss apparently came from the judge at the second hearing.

A different result was reached in *Reynolds* v *British Leyland*, a personal injury claim. After a long delay and without serving a notice of intention to proceed, the plaintiff's solicitor issued a summons to inspect the scene of the accident. The following month the defendants' solicitors enquired by letter whether the action was ready for trial. Both sides attended the hearing of the summons when the application was refused. After a further three months or so the plaintiff took out a summons for directions, ignoring the automatic directions of RSC O 25 r 8. At the hearing about seven weeks later, which the defendants' solicitor did not attend, it was ordered that the action should be set down. The application to dismiss was then issued, an earlier summons for the same relief having been abandoned because only five minutes had been allocated for it to be heard. The action was struck out by the Court of Appeal. Russell LJ felt that there was nothing in the defendants' conduct that could have induced the plaintiff to believe the case would be tried. In particular the letter asking whether the action was ready for trial was "a perfectly natural query" at that stage relevant to the decision whether an application to dismiss should be made, and the defendants' appearance at the plaintiff's summons for inspection was no more than they were entitled and indeed bound to do in the light of what had gone before. Staughton LJ added that since the plaintiff had waited for over three months after that hearing before issuing and serving the summons for direction, there was in any case further unreasonable delay upon which the defendants could rely. In *Harwood* v *Courtaulds Ltd* (1993) the Court of Appeal held that "post-acquiescence" delay by the plaintiff would not entitle the defendants to have the action dismissed unless that further delay caused additional prejudice. In *Armstrong* v *Glofield Properties* a long period of inactivity was ended by a notice of intention to proceed followed by service of the statement of claim. The defendants responded by requesting an extension of time for the defence, and when served it was accompanied by a request for further and better particulars of the statement of claim. The Court of Appeal nevertheless dismissed the action. The serving of a request for further and better particulars might suffice to bar a striking out application but it was for the plaintiff to show that he had incurred further costs as a result of the request in the reasonable belief that the defendant would allow the case to proceed; here there was no evidence of any such belief. In *Draper* v *Ferrymasters Ltd* (1993) the Court of Appeal held that neither continued settlement negotiations nor a payment into court amounted to acquiescence in the delay so as to give rise to an estoppel.

The reasoning of *County & District Properties* v *Lyell* does not have the same force in a case where the plaintiff's delay and the subsequent resumption of proper progress all occur within the limitation period. Given that an application to dismiss is almost always hopeless at that stage, it might be thought that the defendant's actions could not reasonably be taken as an indication that the case will be allowed to proceed. That situation arose in *Simpson* v *Smith* (1989), a personal injury claim arising from an accident which took place when the plaintiff was almost nine. The limitation period expired on 1 June 1988, three years after he attained his majority. There were long delays up to October 1987, but by then the plaintiff had appointed new solicitors and thereafter proper progress was made. The new solicitors applied in November 1987 to set the action down, and that was done later that month. In December the defendant's solicitors applied for a fixed date for trial. The following March they took out the summons to dismiss. Apparently it was served only on 27 June 1988, by which time the limitation period had expired. The Court of Appeal declined to dismiss the proceedings. It was not normally correct to strike out an action where the delay had ceased and proper steps were again being taken. That was so even in a case where the limitation period was still current when progress was resumed. The defendant's application for a fixed date was an active step which probably led the plaintiff's solicitors to believe that the action would go ahead. Otherwise they could have discontinued the proceedings and issued a fresh writ.

(e) Other points

In *Westminster City Council* v *Clifford Culpin* (1987) the Court of Appeal stated that where there is more than one defendant striking-out applications made by two or more should normally be given separate consideration and the relevant principles applied to each in turn. This appears correct since the degree of prejudice suffered by the defendants through the delay may vary. However, in *Hollis* v *Islington London Borough Council* (1989, unreported), also a decision of the Court of Appeal, it was said that an action should only exceptionally be struck out against one defendant and allowed to continue against the others, especially where there are rights of indemnity or contribution among them. Perhaps the correct approach is that the existence of proceedings against other defendants and of possible rights between them is a factor which the court is entitled to take into account in the exercise of its discretion. Without prejudice correspondence relevant to the question of delay or to the conduct of the parties may be admitted on an application to dismiss for want of prosecution, for the general rule excluding such matters is not absolute (*Family Housing Association (Manchester)* v *Michael Hyde & Partners* (1992)). For example, the correspondence may contain an intimation by the defendant that he is willing for the case to proceed in spite of the delay or indicate conduct from which such willingness could be inferred.

The Courts and Legal Services Act 1990 s 102 inserts a new s 13A into the Arbitration Act 1950. This enables an arbitration to be dismissed for want of prosecution unless a contrary intention is expressed in the arbitration agreement. The principles applicable to High Court actions are expressly adopted and by subs (3) the Secretary of State has power to amend the provision in order to keep it in line with any changes in those principles. The section came into force on 1 January 1992. It does not enable an arbitration to be dismissed on the ground of delay occurring solely before that date (*Yamashita-Shinnihon Steamship Co Ltd* v *L'Office Cherifien des Phosphates Unitramp SA* (1993)).

Chapter 14

New claims in pending actions

A fresh claim introducing a new cause of action or joining a new party is frequently made in the course of a pending action, commonly though not always by amendment to the writ or pleadings. If the limitation period relevant to the new claim is still current at that stage no particular problems arise, but where it has expired there are certain special rules. In general there is no reason why a time bar should not avail against a claim made in the course of an action in the same way as against claims pleaded from the start but there are a few exceptional instances where the policy of the law is to allow the limitation defence only where the new claim was already statute-barred when the action was commenced. For proceedings started on or after 1 May 1981 the relevant provisions are contained in the Limitation Act 1980 s 35. By s 40(1) and Sch 2, s 35 does not affect actions begun before that date; these are governed by the common law and in certain respects by Limitation Act 1939 s 28. This chapter is confined to the position under the 1980 Act.

1. The literal meaning of LA 1980 s 35

The effect of s 35 was considered by the Court of Appeal in *Kennett* v *Brown* (1988) which is discussed below. Before that decision it was thought that the section dealt with the problem as follows:

(a) Subsection (2) defines a "new claim" as a claim by way of set-off or counterclaim or a claim involving the addition or substitution of a new cause of action or of a new party.

(b) By subs (1) a new claim is deemed to be a separate action and to have been commenced on the same date as the original action. Thus the introduction of a statute-barred new claim will relate back to the date of issue of the writ and, on the face of it, will defeat any limitation defence which has accrued since that time. This does not apply to claims made in or by way of third party proceedings. These are discussed separately below.

(c) To preserve accrued limitation defences, subs (3) provides that the court must not allow a new claim to be made in the course of an action after the expiry of any time limit under the Act which would affect a new action to enforce that claim. Again this has no application to third party proceedings. There are certain exceptions to subs (3), and these are considered below.

Before *Kennett* v *Brown* it was thought that the effect of s 35 was that, as a general rule, limitation defences to new claims had to be dealt with at the time of the attempted introduction of the new claim into the action; after that, it would be too late. This is certainly the effect of the section taken literally. For example, if a plaintiff obtained leave under RSC O 20 r 5 to make amendments to his statement of claim which raised a fresh cause of action, the amendments would have retrospective effect and the plea of limitation could not succeed unless the new claim was already statute-barred when the writ was issued. It would be incumbent upon the defendant to oppose the application for leave to amend, relying on s 35(3). The court should of course consider the point of its own motion but, if it is not raised, it is likely to go by default. Consequently on this view of the section a mere procedural error by the defendant's solicitors in omitting to oppose the application for leave to amend could have drastic consequences. In instances where the plaintiff can amend without leave under RSC O 20 rr 1 and 3, matters would be even worse as here it is for the defendant to take the initiative by applying under RSC O 20 r 4 for the amendments to be disallowed. The literal construction of s 35 had the further serious disadvantage that the interlocutory procedure is not always appropriate for the resolution of limitation issues. Difficult questions may arise which require pleadings, discovery of documents and a trial for their proper determination. For example, the date of accrual of the cause of action and the date of the plaintiff's knowledge for the purposes of LA 1980 s 14 and s 14A might well be very difficult to determine reliably by the interlocutory process.

2. *Kennett* v *Brown*

The Court of Appeal decided in *Kennett* v *Brown* that s 35(3) is not to be taken literally. The decision has in effect placed severe limitations on the application of the "relation back" principle and as a result has remedied the most serious defects in s 35. The facts were as follows. A collision occurred between two motorcycles in which a pillion passenger on one of them was injured. She sued both drivers. A little more than three years after the accident the first defendant served a contribution notice on the second defendant under RSC O 16 r 8 claiming an indemnity against any liability of his to the plaintiff and also damages for the injuries which he had himself suffered in the collision. When he applied for directions in the contribution proceedings the District Registrar, applying s 35, decided that the personal injury claim could not be put forward unless the first defendant first made a successful application under LA 1980 s 33 to have the normal limitation period disapplied. He adjourned the hearing for that to be done. The decision was overturned by Sir Douglas Frank QC, who gave directions in the contribution proceedings holding that it was for the second defendant to raise the issue of limitation by an appropriate plea and that only then need the first defendant apply under s 33.

The second defendant brought the matter before Lord Donaldson MR and Parker LJ in the Court of Appeal. They upheld the decision of Sir

Douglas Frank. Lord Donaldson, Parker LJ concurring, pointed out that statutes of limitation have almost always operated as procedural bars which apply only if a defendant chooses to raise them. Parliament must be deemed to have been aware of that. The words of s 35(3) "neither the High Court nor any county court shall allow a new claim ... to be made in the course of any action" should therefore not be taken literally any more than the wording of the sections laying down the limitation periods themselves. These typically employ the formula "an action to which this section applies shall not be brought ..." but this merely means that if such an action is brought it shall not succeed. Lord Donaldson's view was that the wording of s 35(3) should receive the same construction. Section 35(1) did not pose any obstacle to this approach. Certainly it meant that the first defendant's claim against the second defendant related back to the date of the writ but that alone did not defeat the defence of limitation. It would prevent the second defendant from relying on the Limitation Act s 11, the main provision governing personal injury claims, but he could plead s 35(3) instead because, subject to the outcome of an application under s 33, the claim was a new claim of the type which by virtue of the subsection the court must not allow. Thus s 35(3) is not to be taken as preventing the introduction of a new claim. Its effect, like that of the other provisions of the Limitation Act, is merely to create a procedural bar which the defendant must plead if he wishes to rely on it. The main result is that the mere introduction of a new claim, other than those excepted from s 35(3), will not serve to defeat the defence of limitation.

(a) New cause of action

If the amendment merely introduces a new cause of action between existing parties it should now be pointless for the defendant even to oppose the plaintiff's application on the ground that the new claim is statute-barred, since according to *Kennett* v *Brown* the limitation defence must first be pleaded. However, it may be that in practice the issue is still frequently considered at the amendment stage. The important difference since *Kennett* v *Brown* is that even after the amendment has been made it remains open to the defendant to plead limitation. Thereafter the procedural possibilities are the same as in the case of issues pleaded from the start. As explained in Chapter 15, these are first to leave the matter to the trial, secondly to have it resolved as a preliminary issue by the trial procedure under RSC O 33 r 3 and r 4(2), and thirdly, in an obvious case, to deal with it by a summons to strike out the statute-barred claim as an abuse of the process of the court under RSC O 18 r 19(1). Whatever procedure is followed, the issues will be whether or not the limitation period applicable to the new claim has expired and, if it expired only after issue of the writ, whether the claim falls within one of the exceptions to s 35(3).

(b) New party

For some time matters seemed to be substantially the same in the case of joinder of a new defendant or plaintiff in spite of RSC O 15 r 6(5). This provides that except in specific circumstances stipulated in the rule, "no person shall be added or substituted as a party after the expiry of any relevant period of limitation". It will be appreciated that *Kennett* v *Brown* did not involve the joinder of a new party but rather contribution proceedings between existing defendants. It was therefore an example of the addition of a new cause of action between existing parties. Nevertheless the decision was applied by the Court of Appeal in *Holland* v *Yates Building Co Ltd* (1989). This concerned a plaintiff's application for leave to join an additional defendant. It was held that it was wrong to seek to determine the question whether or not the cause of action against the new party was statute-barred unless and until the party sought to be joined had pleaded the defence of limitation. The words of RSC O 15 r 6(5) quoted above were not discussed. On this view the proper procedure for a new defendant in these circumstances is to serve a defence pleading limitation. For all practical purposes he then has the same procedural options as if he were an original defendant; see Chapter 15, page 110. There is one slight difference. The new defendant can of course use the interlocutory process to obtain an order that he cease to be a party, but whereas an original defendant would apply under RSC O 18 r 19(1), a defendant joined during the course of the action must rely instead on RSC O 15 r 6(2)(a). However, the Court of Appeal held in *Leicester Wholesale Fruit Market Ltd* v *Grundy* (1990) that the proper test under that rule is whether, if a fresh action had been brought against the new defendant, he could have struck out the proceedings under RSC O 18 r 19(1) as an abuse of the process of the court. The issue is therefore the same in both cases.

This view of matters may no longer be correct because of the decision of the Court of Appeal in *Howe* v *David Brown Tractors (Retail) Ltd* (1991). The plaintiff was injured while using a tractor which had been bought from the defendants by the firm in which he and his father were the partners. In the course of the action he applied to join the firm as second plaintiffs, primarily in order to enable a claim for breach of contract to be made. It was held that this claim was a personal injury claim for limitation purposes and therefore subject to LA 1980 s 11. This aspect of the case is discussed in Chapter 7; see page 42. The three year period of s 11 having elapsed, the issue arose whether the firm could properly be joined in the absence of a direction under LA 1980 s 33 that the limitation period be disapplied. As already mentioned, RSC O 15 r 6(5) provides that no new party may be added or substituted after the expiry of the relevant limitation period. One of the exceptions is where a direction is made under s 33 that the limitation period shall not apply to the claim made by or against the new party. The Court of Appeal held that the firm could not be added as second plaintiffs until such a direction had been given; an application under s 33 had to be made before or at the same time as the application for leave to amend. It was pointed out that RSC O 15 r 6(5) had not been relevant in *Kennett* v *Brown* as that case did not involve an application to join a new party. *Holland* v *Yates Building Co* was not cited but it is difficult to see how the court could have reached any different conclusion except by disregarding RSC O 15 r 6(5) altogether.

Assuming that *Howe* v *David Brown* is correct, the defendant can oppose the plaintiff's summons for leave to amend on the ground that the limitation period has expired. But most cases in this category will be applications to join as a new defendant someone who is not yet a party and who will therefore be unable to oppose the application. Such a defendant can apply under RSC O 12 r 8 within the time limited for service of the defence for an order that he be dismissed from the action (*Liff* v *Peasley* (1980)). Where the amendments are made without leave he can also use RSC O 20 r 4. In practice he will usually rely on RSC O 15 r 6(2)(a) under which the court has a discretion, exercisable at any stage in the proceedings, to order that a person who has been improperly joined should cease to be a party. Alternatively, or in addition, the defendant has the other procedural options available under the *Holland* v *Yates* reasoning, since the decision in *Howe* v *David Brown* does not affect the interpretation put upon s 35(3) in *Kennett* v *Brown* and so limitation can be pleaded in the normal way. That is of course necessary because, in view of *Leicester Wholesale Fruit Market Ltd* v *Grundy*, an application under O 15 r 6(2)(a) will succeed only in a very clear case.

3. The exceptions to s 35(3)

As already mentioned, there are exceptions to the prohibition contained in s 35(3). A new claim falling within one of the exceptions nevertheless has retrospective effect under s 35(1). Consequently it is not vulnerable to the plea of limitation unless it was already statute-barred at the date of the writ. That of course is the intended result. The exceptions are, first, original set-offs and counterclaims, secondly the operation of the Limitation Act s 33, thirdly certain further categories laid down by rules of court. Section 35(4) and (7) create the power to make such rules but provide that they should accord with restrictive conditions contained in subss (5) and (6). These conditions are substantially repeated in the relevant rules of court. Numerous examples of decisions under those rules are given in the notes to RSC O 15 r 6 and O 20 r 5 in *The Supreme Court Practice*.

(a) An original set-off or counterclaim

By s 35(3) a set-off or counterclaim is original if it is made by a party who has not previously made any claim in the action. The existence of this exception prevents a plaintiff from avoiding a set-off or counterclaim by issuing his writ shortly before the end of the limitation period and waiting until its expiry before service. New claims made by amendment to a set-off or counterclaim are of course subject to s 35(3) as they are not original. However, a pure defence is not a set-off or counterclaim and is not subject to any time limit or to s 35 (*Henriksens Rederi* v *THZ Rolimpex* (1973)). Consequently a defendant whose rights have the effect of destroying the plaintiff's cause of action altogether (rather than merely reducing his claim to nil through set-off as a matter of mathematics) can rely on them at any stage, and s 35 does not prevent amendment of the defence.

(b) *Limitation Act s 33*

The operation of s 33 is not affected by s 35. As already mentioned, RSC O 15 r 6(5)(b) permits the addition or substitution of a new party outside the limitation period arising under s 11 or s 12 if the court has directed that those provisions shall not apply to the action by or against the new party. Rather oddly there is no corresponding provision in RSC O 20 r 5 for the addition of a new cause of action against an existing party. However, the point is academic. It does not matter whether this particular case is within s 35(3) or not since once a direction has been made under s 33 the limitation period simply ceases to apply and it will therefore achieve nothing for the defendant to plead it, even assuming s 35(3) permits him to do so. *Kennett* v *Brown* itself was an example of this category of case. Section 33 does not depend on retroactivity. It can therefore be successfully used even where the cause of action was statute-barred at the date of the writ.

(c) *Correction of the name of a party (RSC O 20 r 5(2) and (3))*

An amendment to correct a party's name may be allowed at the court's discretion even though the effect will be to substitute a new party. The court must be satisfied that the mistake was genuine and not misleading or such as to cause any reasonable doubt about the identity of the party in question. The rule is in the same terms as existed before the 1980 Act.

(d) *Alteration in a party's capacity (RSC O 20 r 5(2) and (4))*

An amendment to alter the capacity in which a party sues may be allowed at the court's discretion irrespective of whether the party had that capacity at the commencement of the action or has acquired it subsequently. Thus a widow suing under the Fatal Accidents Act 1976 may be permitted to amend after expiry of the limitation period so as to sue as personal representative under the Law Reform (Miscellaneous Provisions) Act 1934, whether as executrix or administratrix. The power given by the Limitation Act s 35(7) has been used to redraft this rule. Previously it allowed amendment outside the limitation period to alter the capacity of a party who was also an executor, as the executor's title relates back to the date of death of the deceased, but it did not permit such an amendment in the case of an administrator, whose title dates only from the grant of representation. That distinction is now irrelevant.

(e) *A new cause of action arising out of substantially the same facts (RSC O 20 r 5(2) and (5))*

It can sometimes be difficult to say whether an amendment involves a new cause of action or merely clarifies or corrects particulars of an existing cause of action. Where the amendment seeks only to alter a date pleaded in the statement of claim, it is within the latter category as the date is not a material part of the cause of action (*Hay* v *London Brick Co Ltd* (1981)). By contrast, an amendment adding an allegation of negligence to existing allegations of breach of statutory duty should be clearly on the other side of the line. Yet the opposite conclusion was reached in *Dornan* v *JW Ellis & Co Ltd* (1962), though the rules were in different terms at the time. Where the amendment does involve a new cause of action, it may be permitted under RSC O 20 r 5 provided that facts as a cause of action already pleaded by the amending party. This rule is in the same terms as before the 1980 Act. In *Sayer* v *Kingston & Esher Health Authority* (1989) the Court of Appeal held that the use of the expression "substantially the same facts" meant that the discretion existed even in a case where the amending party would have to rely on facts not relevant to the issues pleaded originally in order to establish the new claim. The plaintiff's original case related to alleged negligence at the time of her caesarian operation in the defendant's hospital. Outside the limitation period she wished to make amendments which for the most part concerned the treatment she received in the period after the operation and which in fact deleted the complaints the new cause of action arose out of the same or substantially the same about the caesarian section altogether. The amendments were held to fall within RSC O 20 r 5(5). The new cause of action arose out of substantially the same facts as that pleaded originally. The facts were those relating to the birth of the plaintiff's child, and in the view of the court it would have been unrealistic to compartmentalise that event into a number of different parts. Similarly in *Brickfield Properties Ltd* v *Newton* (1971) a cause of action based on an architect's negligence in the design of a building was held to arise out of the same or substantially the same facts as a cause of action based on his negligence in the supervision of its construction.

It should be remembered that the rules of court do no more than create a discretion. Thus amendments introducing a new cause of action arising out of substantially the same facts as a cause of action already pleaded might be considered unacceptable because the lapse of time since the relevant events has made it impossible for the defendant to mount an effective defence to the new claim. The court may take account of any prejudice which the plaintiff's failure to plead the claim from the start causes the defendant, whether or not the prejudice results from such of the delay as occurs after expiry of the limitation period (*Hancock Shipping Co Ltd* v *Kawasaki Heavy Industries Ltd* (1991)).

(f) Addition or substitution of a new party necessary to the action (RSC O 15 r 6(2)(b), r 6(5)(a) and r 6(6))

A new party may be added or substituted at the court's discretion provided that this is necessary for the determination of the action and that the limitation period was still current when the proceedings were commenced. An exhaustive list of the circumstances in which the addition or substitution is to be treated as necessary is contained in r 6(6). In effect it must be the case that a claim made in the original pleadings cannot be properly resolved otherwise.

4. Third party proceedings

For these purposes third party proceedings are proceedings brought by an existing party against someone not previously a party "other than proceedings brought by joining any such person as defendant to any claim already made in the original action by the party bringing the proceedings" (s 35(2)). Third party proceedings are outside the scope of s 35(3), and the section therefore did not prevent their issue outside the limitation period even before the decision in *Kennett* v *Brown*. Neither is RSC O 15 r 6(5) treated as having that result. The practice where a claim raised by a third party notice is allegedly statute-barred is the same as that relating to claims made by an unamended writ or statement of claim, and the claim can be struck out on an interlocutory application under RSC O 18 r 19(1) in only a very clear case (*Ronex Properties Ltd* v *John Laing Construction Ltd* (1982)). By s 35(1) the commencement of third party proceedings is not retrospective and the third party can therefore simply plead limitation in the normal way. However, by s 35(8) new claims made in the course of third party proceedings relate back to the date of commencement of those proceedings and subss (3) to (7) apply. Third party proceedings are thus treated for these purposes as if they were a separate action. They are commenced on the sealing of the third party notice (RSC O 16 r 3(4)).

5. Further practical points

(a) It is clear that contribution proceedings between existing defendants are not within the definition of third party proceedings contained in s 35(2). This may be an error of drafting. Suppose that in an action involving two defendants the first defendant issues a contribution notice against the second defendant who then responds with a counterclaim, but both claims are made outside the limitation period. The first defendant's claim will be defeated by the plea of limitation but the second defendant's claim, as an original counterclaim, will relate back under s 35(1) not to the date of the first defendant's contribution notice but to the date of the writ, thus defeating any limitation defence which has accrued since that time. In *Kennett* v *Brown* the first defendant had in fact been served with a contribution notice by the second defendant before he himself served the notice which was the subject matter of the decision. However, Lord Donaldson considered that it was not an original counterclaim since that, in his view, was a counterclaim made by an original defendant against an original plaintiff. That part of the decision does not accord with the meaning given to the word "original" by s 35(3).

(b) The position where a party is joined outside the limitation period has already been explained. The exact date of joinder is determined by RSC O 15 r 8(4)(a) which states that where a person is to be added as a party to an action, he shall not become a party until the writ has been amended in relation to him "and (if he is a defendant) has been served on him". In *Ketteman* v *Hansel Properties* (1987) it was held that these words meant exactly what they said. That decision was applied in the context of LA 1980 s 35 in *Bank of America National Trust and Savings Association* v *Chrismas* (1992). Thus a plaintiff who amends to add a new defendant must not only make the amendments but also serve the new party before expiry of the limitation period.

There is some doubt about the effective date of amendments introducing a new cause of action between existing parties. The possibilities are the date of issue of the summons for leave, the date of the order granting leave and the date the amendments themselves are actually made. In *Firman* v *Ellis* (1978) the Court of Appeal assumed that the amendments would be effective as from the date of the order. Again a fresh writ will be necessary if a hearing date before the end of the limitation period cannot be obtained.

(c) By s 39 the 1980 Act does not apply to an action for which the limitation period is prescribed by another enactment. In such cases the effect of a new claim is therefore governed by the common law. In *Ketteman* v *Hansel Properties* (1987) the House of Lords held unanimously that the joinder of a new defendant did not have retrospective effect at common law, and there is no reason to think that an amendment introducing a new cause of action between existing parties would be treated any differently. New claims are therefore dealt with in the same way as those pleaded from the start. Unfortunately this must apply equally to those new claims which would be excepted from LA 1980 s 35(3) in actions governed by the 1980 Act (though not the exercise of the discretion under LA 1980 s 33, which is confined to 1980 Act cases anyway). Consequently it will not assist the amending party to show that the new claim is within one of the excepted categories.

(d) Matters are less clear where the limitation period is contractual. There are conflicting first instance decisions. The issue is whether or not s 35 applies at all in such cases. If it does, the new claim will have retrospective effect under s 35(1). Thanks to *Kennett* v *Brown* s 35(3) normally permits limitation to be pleaded anyway, but the subsection does not extend to contractual limitation periods. It enjoins the court not to allow a new claim "after the expiry of any time limit *under this Act* which would affect a new action to enforce that claim". (Author's italics.) As a result, a limitation defence accruing since the date of the writ would be defeated unless the amendment itself were disallowed. That reasoning was applied in *Katzenstein Adler Industries (1975) Ltd* v

Borchard Lines Ltd (1988). This is of course the procedural trap which *Kennett* v *Brown* removed in other contexts. *Casillo Grani* v *Napier Shipping Co* (1984) was also decided on the basis that the question of retroactivity is to be determined by s 35, though the actual result of the case was different for reasons explained below. The view taken by Hobhouse J in *Payabi* v *Armstell Shipping Corp* (1992) seems preferable. This is that even s 35(1) has no application to contractual time limits because it begins with the words "For the purposes of this Act ...", so that new claims have retrospective effect only for the purposes of the limitation periods laid down by the 1980 Act. Since the common law does not give the new claim retrospective effect (*Ketteman* v *Hansel Properties*), the consequences of this reasoning are the same as in the case of time limits created by other statutes (above, point (c)). The proposition that the question of retroactivity is to be decided under the common law rather than the Act is supported by *Empresa Cubana Importadora de Alimentos* v *Octavier Shipping Co SA* (1986). All these cases concerned the Hague Visby Rules, which were incorporated into the bills of lading in each case. This creates a further complication because the Hague Visby Rules have the force of law by virtue of the Carriage of Goods by Sea Act 1971, and under Article X their application extends to cases where the bill of lading provides that they are to govern the contract. They thus have statutory as well as contractual force, and what was said above (point (c)) in relation to LA 1980 s 39 should therefore apply. That reasoning was adopted in *Transworld Oil (USA) Inc* v *Minos Companiera Naviera SA* (1992).

(e) Some of the time bars of the Limitation Act 1980 operate to extinguish the plaintiff's cause of action. They are mentioned in Chapter 15; see page 109. Time bars under certain other statutes have the same effect, and this is true in particular of the Hague Visby Rules. In *Payabi* v *Armstell Shipping Corp* Hobhouse J held that if s 35 did apply then RSC O 20 r 5 should in any event be construed as referring only to procedural bars. It did not extend to time limits which extinguished the cause of action. If it did it would be *ultra vires* as the power under which the rule was made could not deprive a person of an accrued substantive right or, more precisely in the context of the litigation before him, create a substantive cause of action out of nothing, the original cause of action having been extinguished. The same reasoning was applied in *Transworld Oil* v *Minos Companiera Naviera*. In *Casillo Grani* v *Napier Shipping* it was held that although the amendment did have retrospective effect under s 35, this did not operate to resurrect an extinguished cause of action. By contrast the decision in *Empresa Cubana Importadora* v *Octavier Shipping* was that the defunct cause of action was indeed revived in that way. The argument that the rules of court cannot as a matter of law override substantive time bars seems misplaced. It is LA 1980 s 35(1) which, if it applies at all, enables the amendment to defeat the time bar. However, the point of construction remains. Both RSC O 20 r 5 and O 15 r 6(5) refer to periods of limitation, and strictly this term does not include substantive time bars.

As already mentioned, the provisions of the Hague Visby Rules had both statutory and contractual force in the cases discussed. It is not clear whether a purely contractual time bar can operate to extinguish a cause of action. In principle there seems to be no reason why it should not if that were its intended effect as a matter of construction. However, this will be of only academic interest for these purposes if the decision in *Payabi* v *Armstell Shipping* is correct on the contract point.

(f) In county court proceedings the High Court rules relating to amendment are adopted by CCR O 15 r 1. The Limitation Act s 35 of course applies in both High Court and county court proceedings.

(g) Section 35 applies to arbitrations in the same way as to High Court actions (s 34(1)). It also applies to foreign limitation periods to which effect is given by virtue of Foreign Limitation Periods Act 1984 s 1 (1984 Act s 3(1)).

Chapter 15

Other procedural matters

1. The effect of the statute

With three exceptions the time limits laid down by Limitation Act 1980 are procedural rather than substantive, and therefore merely bar the remedy rather than extinguish the right on which the claim is based. The exceptions are s 3(2) (title to chattels), s 17 (title to land) and s 11A(3) (ten year long-stop of Consumer Protection Act 1987). The fifteen year long-stop applicable in negligence actions under s 14B bars the remedy only. There are of course many other statutes which create time bars. The most important are mentioned in Chapter 2; see page 6. Some of these operate to extinguish the cause of action altogether. In particular that is the effect of the Hague Visby Rules, which are contained in the schedule to the Carriage of Goods by Sea Act 1971 (*Aries Tanker Corp* v *Total Transport Ltd* (1977)).

In the normal case, therefore, the limitation period does not affect the plaintiff's rights but removes the means of enforcing them through the courts. The 1980 Act provides that the actions to which it applies "shall not be brought" after their respective limitation periods. By s 38(1) "action" includes any proceedings in a court of law and therefore extends to counterclaims and set-offs. However, the Act does not prevent the enforcement of rights by such other means as may be available. The main consequences of this are as follows:

(a) A creditor who has a lien or other security may enforce the security otherwise than by proceedings even though the debt itself has become statute-barred (*Spears* v *Hartley* (1800), *Re Brockman* (1909)). Thus statute-barred arrears of interest are recoverable by a mortgagee on redemption of the mortgage or following the exercise of his power of sale (*Edmunds* v *Waugh* (1866), *Holmes* v *Cowcher* (1970)).

(b) A bankruptcy or winding-up petition is an "action" for the purposes of the 1980 Act and therefore cannot be founded on a statute-barred debt if the expiry of the limitation period is raised. Neither is such a debt provable in a bankruptcy or liquidation (*ex parte Dewdney* (1809), *Re General Rolling Stock Co* (1872)). However, the contributories may consent to the payment of the debt in a voluntary winding-up of a solvent company (*Re Art Reproduction Co Ltd* (1952)).

(c) Where a debtor pays money without appropriating it to any particular debt, the creditor may himself appropriate it to a statute-barred debt (*Mills* v *Fowkes* (1839)).

(d) A personal representative may deduct the amount of a statute-barred debt from payment of a pecuniary or residuary legacy (*Courtenay* v *Williams* (1844), *Re Akerman* (1891), *Re Cordwell* (1875)).

(e) A personal representative may pay a statute-barred debt, including a debt due to the personal representative himself, without committing a devastavit (*Re Rownson* (1885), *Hill* v *Walker* (1858)). But this does not apply if the debt has been declared barred by a court (*Midgley* v *Midgley* (1893)). Similarly a personal representative is not obliged to plead the statute against a creditor of the estate unless required to do so by another creditor or by a beneficiary (*ex parte Dewdney*).

2. Pleadings

On the face of it the statement of claim should not mention the question of limitation since that would involve anticipating the defence and alleging facts not yet material. If the defence does raise the issue the plaintiff can serve a reply if necessary. However, *The Supreme Court Practice* states (RSC O 18/8/16) that a personal injury plaintiff who wishes to rely on the date of knowledge provisions of LA 1980 s 11 to s 14 must plead the relevant facts in his statement of claim, particularly the respective dates when he first had knowledge of the facts specified in s 14. If he intends to invoke s 33, then unless he has good reason to believe that the defence of limitation will not be raised he should include in his prayer a claim for a direction under the section and again plead all matters relevant. Presumably a similar approach should be taken in negligence actions falling within LA s 14A. It seems that an acknowledgement or part-payment of a statute-barred debt must be pleaded from the start because the effect of s 29(5) is that the right of action is treated as having accrued "on and not before" the date of the acknowledgement or payment. The plea is therefore necessary to establish the plaintiff's true case (*Busch* v *Stevens* (1963)).

The defendant will not be able to rely on a statutory time bar unless he has pleaded its effect (RSC O 18 r 8(1)). Failure to do so may cost him the action. Again *The Supreme Court Practice* suggests (RSC O 18/8/16) that a defendant should serve a detailed pleading in a personal injury action where he wishes to set up a positive case of his own rather than a mere denial of the plaintiff's factual allegations in relation to the date of knowledge or s 33. A party alleging knowledge in a person may be ordered to serve particulars of the facts relied on (RSC O 18 r 12(4)(a)).

3. Methods of disposal of the question of limitation

The limitation question can of course simply be left to the trial and dealt with at the same time as the other matters in dispute. If convenient it may be resolved by the trial procedure as a preliminary issue under RSC O 33 rr 3 and 4(2). Even where it is clear that the plaintiff has no arguable case it cannot be said that the statement of claim discloses no reasonable cause of action (for the purposes of RSC O 18 r 19(1)(a)), as the expiry of the limitation period leaves the cause of action unaffected (*Dismore* v *Milton* (1938)). Matters would no doubt be different in the three instances where the statute extinguishes the claim itself if the expiry of time were apparent from the statement of claim. However, the point is academic in any event because once the defendant has pleaded limitation he can take out a summons for the action to be dismissed under RSC O 18 r 19(1)(b) and (d) as frivolous and vexatious and an abuse of the process of the court, though he will succeed only in a very clear case (*Riches* v *Director of Public Prosecutions* (1973), *Ronex Properties Ltd* v *John Laing Construction Ltd* (1983)). This procedure may also be used where only the equitable doctrine of laches applies (*Gapp* v *Chamberlain* (1991)).

An application under LA s 33 can be dealt with at the trial of the action or as a preliminary issue. Alternatively the plaintiff can use the interlocutory procedure at any stage though in some actions it will be sensible for him to wait until after discovery of documents. In *Firman* v *Ellis* (1978) Lord Denning considered that only a judge could hear such an application, but jurisdiction has since been extended to Masters and District Judges of the High Court (RSC O 32 r 9A). An order giving or refusing a direction under s 33 is a final order for the purposes of RSC O 59 r 1A(3) so that leave is not required for an appeal (*Dale* v *British Coal Corp* (1993)).

4. Onus of proof

Occasionally the evidence will not establish on the balance of probabilities whether the cause of action accrued, or the date of knowledge occurred, within or before the limitation period (reckoning back in time from the date of the writ). The issue will then turn on the onus of proof. In *Cartledge* v *Jopling* the Court of Appeal held that the burden was on the plaintiff to show accrual of his cause of action within the statutory period. The point was not argued in the House of Lords but Lord Pearce, with whom the other members of the Judicial Committee all agreed, added the "gloss" that once the plaintiff proves an occurrence of damage within the period the burden passes to the defendant to show that this is misleading and that in reality the cause of action accrued at an earlier date. It is not clear that this adds anything of substance, but the rule as thus stated was applied by the Court of Appeal in *London Congregational Union Inc* v *Harriss & Harriss* (1988). There have occasionally been judicial statements to different effect, for example in *Fowell* v *National Coal Board*, but these must be regarded as incorrect.

5. Renewal of writs and summonses

For the purpose of service a writ or summons is valid in the first instance for four months, though the court has power to extend its validity for a further period, normally no greater than four months (RSC O 6 r 8, CCR O 7 r 20). More than one application for extension can be made. The wording of RSC O 6 r 8(1) ("four months beginning with the date of its issue") requires the day of service to be counted in the computation of the period (*Trow* v *Ind Coope (West Midlands) Ltd* (1967)). Thus a writ issued on 10 January is valid for service on 9 May but no later. RSC O 6 r 8 applies to an originating summons in the same way as to a writ (RSC O 7 r 6).

The nature of the court's discretion to extend the validity of a writ was considered by the House of Lords in *Kleinwort Benson Ltd* v *Barbrak Ltd* (1987) and *Waddon* v *Whitecroft Scovell Ltd* (1988). In both cases Lord Brandon gave the only speech. It was decided in *Kleinwort Benson Ltd* v *Barbrak Ltd* that on the true construction of RSC O 6 r 8(2) the power should only be exercised for good reason but that it was not confined to cases where there were exceptional circumstances. This resolved a conflict in the earlier authorities. The question whether good reason exists depends on the circumstances of the particular case, and since the decision is discretionary the grounds on which an appellate court can properly interfere are narrow.

The House of Lords was concerned in particular with the principles which should apply in cases involving limitation issues. The general position is that the discretion will not be exercised in such a way as to deprive the defendant of an accrued right of limitation (*Battersby* v *Anglo American Oil Co Ltd* (1945), *Heaven* v *Road and Rail Wagons Ltd* (1965), *The Mouna* (1991)). In normal circumstances this will be sufficient on its own to defeat the application. The plaintiff may nevertheless establish good reason, but something out of the ordinary would be required for that purpose. In *Wilkinson* v *Ancliff (BLT) Ltd* (1986) the Court of Appeal held that the application should be refused even though the defendant could show no more than a reasonably arguable case that he would otherwise be deprived of the defence of limitation. In the absence of special circumstances it was sufficient that there was a real likelihood or substantial risk that the defendant would be prejudiced in that way.

The cases appear to fall into four categories:

(i) the writ is still valid at the time of the application and the limitation period is still current;
(ii) the writ is still valid but the limitation period has expired;
(iii) the writ has ceased to be valid and the limitation period has expired;
(iv) the writ has ceased to be valid but the limitation period is still current.

In *Kleinwort Benson* v *Barbrak* Lord Brandon identified the first three of these as the main categories in which limitation issues may arise. He pointed out that it was only in category (iii) cases that the exercise of the discretion would defeat an accrued right of limitation. Category (ii) cases differed because there it was still possible for the plaintiff to serve the writ in time and thus defeat the limitation defence. But even in category (ii) an extension might enable the plaintiff to serve the writ more than twelve months after expiry of the limitation period. That was a relevant factor because the defendant was entitled to rely on the general rule that a writ against him must be issued within the limitation period and served no more than twelve months later. (Before 4 June 1990 the period laid down by RSC O 6 r 8 was twelve months.)

In *Waddon* v *Whitecroft Scovell* it was argued that personal injury claims should be governed by different principles. The plaintiff contended that the court should make the decision in the same way as in the case of an application under LA 1980 s 33, taking into account the matters to which regard must be had under that provision. The result of that approach would be that renewal would be permitted if the circumstances were such that, assuming the plaintiff had issued his writ outside the limitation period, an application under s 33 would succeed. Lord Brandon rejected this argument because the reasons for not serving a writ issued in time and the reasons for not issuing a writ in time might differ widely. He accepted, however, that there could be cases where the discretion under RSC O 6 r 8 and the discretion under s 33 might fall to be exercised on very similar grounds. The Court of Appeal had already taken a very similar approach in *Player* v *Bruguiere* (1980). In view of the decision in *Walkley* v *Precision Forgings Ltd* (1979), discussed in Chapter 7 (see page 50), the consequence of the rejection of the plaintiff's renewal application in a personal injury claim will almost always be that the action will fail altogether if the primary limitation period has expired at that stage. In *Dagnell* v *Freedman* (1993) the House of Lords held that the state of affairs in related litigation did not constitute good reason for the purposes of RSC O 6 r 8. But the following factors, as well as those already mentioned, have carried some weight:

(a) The defendant's consent to deferment of service or to an extension of validity of the writ (*The Mouna* (1991), *re Chittenden* (1970)). Such an agreement may sometimes be implied (*Hare* v *Personal Representatives of Mohammed Yunis Malik, deceased* (1980)). Or it might be inferred where the defendant has led the plaintiff to believe that the defendant consented or would consent, but the mere fact that settlement negotiations are in progress is insufficient (*The Mouna*). However, the decision is strictly one for the court rather than the parties, and if the defendant agrees that the action should not be prosecuted for the time being, it would be safer for the writ to be served and acknowledged and for time for service of the statement of claim then to be extended by agreement.

(b) Difficulty in effecting service arising without fault on the plaintiff's part, particularly the fact that the defendant has evaded service (*Battersby* v *Anglo American Oil Co Ltd*, *Heaven* v *Road and Rail Wagons Ltd*, *Waddon* v *Whitecroft Scovell Ltd*).

(c) Conduct by the defendant or his representatives which causes or contributes to the delay (*Heaven* v *Road and Rail Wagons Ltd*).

(d) Delays through the operation of the legal aid system. In *Waddon* v *Whitecroft Scovell Ltd dicta* to the opposite effect in two earlier cases were disapproved.

(e) A desire to save unnecessary proceedings and legal costs without any disadvantage to the defendant (*Kleinwort Benson Ltd* v *Barbrak Ltd*), though the circumstances of that case (a very large number of defendants) were "wholly exceptional".

(f) The balance between the hardship to the plaintiff if the application is refused and to the defendant if it is allowed (*Jones* v *Jones* (1970), approved in *Kleinwort Benson Ltd* v *Barbrak Ltd*). In *Waddon* v *Whitecroft Scovell* Lord Brandon explained that this could not of itself be a sufficient reason for extending the validity of a writ but where there were matters potentially capable of constituting good reason, the balance of hardship might then be relevant to the decision.

In the great majority of cases the plaintiff is unlikely to be able to show good reason for an extension unless he can also show good reason for his failure to serve the writ, and in particular that this was not due to any fault on his part. In *Kleinwort Benson* v *Barbrak* Lord Brandon pointed out that in category (iii) cases (writ expired, limitation period expired) the plaintiff must also give a satisfactory explanation for his failure to apply for an extension while the writ was still valid. The same would of course apply to category (iv) (writ expired, limitation period still current). In *Waddon* v *Whitecroft Scovell* Lord Brandon stressed that it was the plaintiff's solicitor's duty to make full and frank disclosure of all relevant matters, the application being made *ex parte*, and that the question whether the limitation period had expired or would expire shortly was crucial.

Where the limitation period is still current (categories (i) and (iv)), a plaintiff's solicitor might be well advised to issue a second writ rather than seek to extend the validity of the first. The *ex parte* order cannot safely be relied on since after service it is open to the defendant to apply under RSC O 12 r 8 for it to be discharged and for service of the writ to be set aside on the grounds that there was no good reason for the extension. Such an outcome would be fatal to the plaintiff's position if the limitation period had expired in the meanwhile. The issue of a fresh writ avoids this risk and in some cases would be both simpler and cheaper anyway. The gravity of the risk is dramatically illustrated by *Waddon* v *Whitecroft Scovell*, which was an example of category (ii). The writ was issued on 29 November 1982 and the limitation period expired shortly afterwards. The application to extend was lodged on 9 November 1983. By then the plaintiff's legal aid certificate covered the obtaining of evidence and counsel's opinion and the issue of a writ but not its service. His solicitors were waiting for a report from a firm of engineering consultants. As it happened, it came to hand on 18 November 1983. Their application was heard on 23 November. The defendants' subsequent summons for an order setting service aside succeeded mainly, if not entirely, because in the ten days between receipt of the expert's report and the expiry of the writ the plaintiff's solicitors omitted to apply to the legal aid area office for removal of the restriction on their client's certificate. Had they done so, service might have been effected within the original period of validity of the writ. If an application for amendment of the certificate had been made but not granted in time, that could have been taken into account—but it had not happened. It made no difference that the defendants and their insurers might not have been prejudiced by the delay in service, being already fully aware of the plaintiff's claim, because the balance of hardship between the parties was relevant only where there were other matters which could potentially constitute good reason within RSC O 6 r 8. It is worth adding that although the plaintiff's solicitors had ten days after receipt of the engineer's report before expiry of the writ, they had only from 18 November to 23 November before the hearing of their application. That period included a weekend. The failure to serve the writ in the five days following the hearing could not be relevant to the existence of good reason at the time of the hearing. In any event the writ was lost in the District Registry at that stage and finally returned, freshly dated, only on 26 March 1984.

The risk may be present even where the limitation period is still current at the time of the application and the writ is served before its expiry, since the crucial factor will be whether the period has expired at the time of the hearing of the defendant's summons under RSC O 12 r 8. Ironically the effect of setting aside service in those circumstances would be to present the defendant with a limitation defence which he would not otherwise have. Clearly an application to extend the validity of a writ or summons should be regarded as a last resort.

The idea has been mooted more than once that to defeat the defence of limitation the proceedings should be both issued and served within the statutory period. The Courts and Legal Services Bill contained a clause to that effect but it did not survive into the Act.

Appendix 1

Limitation Act 1980

ARRANGEMENT OF SECTIONS

PART I

ORDINARY TIME LIMITS FOR DIFFERENT CLASSES OF ACTION

Time limits under Part I subject to extension or exclusion under Part II

Section

1 Time limits under Part I subject to extension or exclusion under Part II.

Actions founded on tort

2 Time limit for actions founded on tort.
3 Time limit in case of successive conversions and extinction of title of owner of converted goods.
4 Special time limit in case of theft.
4A Time limits for actions for libel and slander.

Actions founded on simple contract

5 Time limit for actions founded on simple contract.
6 Special time limit for actions in respect of certain loans.
7 Time limit for actions to enforce certain awards.

General rule for actions on a specialty

8 Time limit for actions on a specialty.

Actions for sums recoverable by statute

9 Time limit for actions for sums recoverable by statute.
10 Special time limit for claiming contribution.

Actions in respect of wrongs causing personal injuries or death

11 Special time limit for actions in respect of personal injuries.
11A Actions in respect of defective products.
12 Special time limit for actions under Fatal Accidents legislation.
13 Operation of time limit under section 12 in relation to different dependants.
14 Definition of date of knowledge for purposes of sections 11 and 12.

Actions in respect of latent damage not involving personal injuries

Section
14A Special time limit for negligence actions where facts relevant to cause of action are not known at date of accrual.
14B Overriding time limit for negligence actions not involving personal injuries.

Actions to recover land and rent

15 Time limit for action to recover land.
16 Time limit for redemption actions.
17 Extinction of title to land after expiration of time limit.
18 Settled land and land held on trust.
19 Time limit for actions to recover rent.

Actions to recover money secured by a mortgage or charge or to recover proceeds of the sale of land

20 Time limit for actions to recover money secured by a mortgage or charge or to recover proceeds of the sale of land.

Actions in respect of trust property or the personal estate of deceased persons

21 Time limit for actions in respect of trust property.
22 Time limit for actions claiming personal estate of a deceased person.

Actions for an account

23 Time limit in respect of actions for an account.

Miscellaneous and supplemental

24 Time limit for actions to enforce judgments.
25 Time limit for actions to enforce advowsons and extinction of title to advowsons.
26 Administration to date back to death.
27 Cure of defective disentailing assurance.

PART II

EXTENSION OR EXCLUSION OF ORDINARY TIME LIMITS

Disability

Section
28 Extension of limitation period in case of disability.
28A Extension for cases where the limitation period is the period under section 14A(4)(*b*).

Acknowledgment and part payment

29 Fresh accrual of action on acknowledgment or part payment.
30 Formal provisions as to acknowledgments and part payments.
31 Effect of acknowledgment or part payment on persons other than the maker or recipient.

Appendix 1

An Act to consolidate the Limitation Acts 1939 to 1980.

[13th November 1980]

Act extended by Water Act 1981, s 6(4)

PART I

ORDINARY TIME LIMITS FOR DIFFERENT CLASSES OF ACTION

Time limits under Part I subject to extension or exclusion under Part II

1 Time limits under Part I subject to extension or exclusion under Part II

(1) This Part of this Act gives the ordinary time limits for bringing actions of the various classes mentioned in the following provisions of this Part.

(2) The ordinary time limits given in this Part of this Act are subject to extension or exclusion in accordance with the provisions of Part II of this Act.

Actions founded on tort

2 Time limit for actions founded on tort

An action founded on tort shall not be brought after the expiration of six years from the date on which the cause of action accrued.

3 Time limit in case of successive conversions and extinction of title of owner of converted goods

(1) Where any cause of action in respect of the conversion of a chattel has accrued to any person and, before he recovers possession of the chattel, a further conversion takes place, no action shall be brought in respect of the further conversion after the expiration of six years from the accrual of the cause of action in respect of the original conversion.

(2) Where any such cause of action has accrued to any person and the period prescribed for bringing that action has expired and he has not during that period recovered possession of the chattel, the title of that person to the chattel shall be extinguished.

4 Special time limit in case of theft

(1) The right of any person from whom a chattel is stolen to bring an action in respect of the theft shall not be subject to the time limits under sections 2 and 3(1) of this Act, but if his title to the chattel is extinguished under section 3(2) of this Act he may not bring an action in respect of a theft preceding the loss of his title, unless the theft in question preceded the conversion from which time began to run for the purposes of section 3(2).

(2) Subsection (1) above shall apply to any conversion related to the theft of a chattel as it applies to the theft of a chattel; and, except as provided below, every conversion following the theft of a chattel before the person from whom it is stolen recovers possession of it shall be regarded for the purposes of this section as related to the theft.

If anyone purchases the stolen chattel in good faith neither the purchase nor any conversion following it shall be regarded as related to the theft.

(3) Any cause of action accruing in respect of the theft or any conversion related to the theft of a chattel to any person from whom the chattel is stolen shall be disregarded for the purpose of applying section 3(1) or (2) of this Act to his case.

(4) Where in any action brought in respect of the conversion of a chattel it is proved that the chattel was stolen from the plaintiff or anyone through whom he claims it shall be presumed that any conversion following the theft is related to the theft unless the contrary is shown.

(5) In this section "theft" includes—

(*a*) any conduct outside England and Wales which would be theft if committed in England and Wales; and
(*b*) obtaining any chattel (in England and Wales or elsewhere) in the circumstances described in section 15(1) of the Theft Act 1968 (obtaining by deception) or by blackmail within the meaning of section 21 of that Act;

and references in this section to a chattel being "stolen" shall be construed accordingly.

[4A Time limit for actions for libel or slander

The time limit under section 2 of this Act shall not apply to an action for libel or slander, but no such action shall be brought after the expiration of three years from the date on which the cause of action accrued.][1]

1 Inserted by the Administration of Justice Act 1985, ss 57(2), 69(5), 9 Sch 14.

Actions founded on simple contract

5 Time limit for actions founded on simple contract

An action founded on simple contract shall not be brought after the expiration of six years from the date on which the cause of action accrued.

6 Special time limit for actions in respect of certain loans

(1) Subject to subsection (3) below, section 5 of this Act shall not bar the right of action on a contract of loan to which this section applies.

(2) This section applies to any contract of loan which—

(*a*) does not provide for repayment of the debt on or before a fixed or determinable date; and
(*b*) does not effectively (whether or not it purports to do so) make the obligation to repay the debt conditional on a demand for repayment made by or on behalf of the creditor or on any other matter;

except where in connection with taking the loan the debtor enters into any collateral obligation to pay the amount of the debt or any part of it (as, for example, by delivering a promissory note as security for the debt) on terms which would exclude the application of this section to the contract of loan if they applied directly to repayment of the debt.

(3) Where a demand in writing for repayment of the debt under a contract of loan to which this section applies is made by or on behalf of the creditor (or, where there are joint creditors, by or on behalf of any one of them) section 5 of

this Act shall thereupon apply as if the cause of action to recover the debt had accrued on the date on which the demand was made.

(4) In this section "promissory note" has the same meaning as in the Bills of Exchange Act 1882.

7 Time limit for actions to enforce certain awards

An action to enforce an award, where the submission is not by an instrument under seal, shall not be brought after the expiration of six years from the date on which the cause of action accrued.

General rule for actions on a specialty

8 Time limit for actions on a specialty

(1) An action upon a specialty shall not be brought after the expiration of twelve years from the date on which the cause of action accrued.

(2) Subsection (1) above shall not affect any action for which a shorter period of limitation is prescribed by any other provision of this Act.

Actions for sums recoverable by statute

9 Time limit for actions for sums recoverable by statute

(1) An action to recover any sum recoverable by virtue of any enactment shall not be brought after the expiration of six years from the date on which the cause of action accrued.

(2) Subsection (1) above shall not affect any action to which section 10 of this Act applies.

10 Special time limit for claiming contribution

(1) Where under section 1 of the Civil Liability (Contribution) Act 1978 any person becomes entitled to a right to recover contribution in respect of any damage from any other person, no action to recover contribution by virtue of that right shall be brought after the expiration of two years from the date on which that right accrued.

(2) For the purposes of this section the date on which a right to recover contribution in respect of any damage accrues to any person (referred to below in this section as "the relevant date") shall be ascertained as provided in subsections (3) and (4) below.

(3) If the person in question is held liable in respect of that damage—

(*a*) by a judgment given in any civil proceedings; or
(*b*) by an award made on any arbitration;

the relevant date shall be the date on which the judgment is given, or the date of the award (as the case may be).

For the purposes of this subsection no account shall be taken of any judgment or award given or made on appeal in so far as it varies the amount of damages awarded against the person in question.

(4) If, in any case not within subsection (3) above, the person in question makes or agrees to make any payment to one or more persons in compensation for that damage (whether he admits any liability in respect of the damage or

not), the relevant date shall be the earliest date on which the amount to be paid by him is agreed between him (or his representative) and the person (or each of the persons, as the case may be) to whom the payment is to be made.

(5) An action to recover contribution shall be one to which sections 28, 32 and 35 of this Act apply, but otherwise Parts II and III of this Act (except sections 34, 37 and 38) shall not apply for the purposes of this section.

Actions in respect of wrongs causing personal injuries or death

11 Special time limit for actions in respect of personal injuries

(1) This section applies to any action for damages for negligence, nuisance or breach of duty (whether the duty exists by virtue of a contract or of provision made by or under a statute or independently of any contract or any such provision) where the damages claimed by the plaintiff for the negligence, nuisance or breach of duty consist of or include damages in respect of personal injuries to the plaintiff or any other person.

(2) None of the time limits given in the preceding provisions of this Act shall apply to an action to which this section applies.

(3) An action to which this section applies shall not be brought after the expiration of the period applicable in accordance with subsection (4) or (5) below.

(4) Except where subsection (5) below applies, the period applicable is three years from—

(*a*) the date on which the cause of action accrued; or
(*b*) the date of knowledge (if later) of the person injured.

(5) If the person injured dies before the expiration of the period mentioned in subsection (4) above, the period applicable as respects the cause of action surviving for the benefit of his estate by virtue of section 1 of the Law Reform (Miscellaneous Provisions) Act 1934 shall be three years from—

(*a*) the date of death; or
(*b*) the date of the personal representative's knowledge;

whichever is the later.

(6) For the purposes of this section "personal representative" includes any person who is or has been a personal representative of the deceased, including an executor who has not proved the will (whether or not he has renounced probate) but not anyone appointed only as a special personal representative in relation to settled land; and regard shall be had to any knowledge acquired by any such person while a personal representative or previously.

(7) If there is more than one personal representative, and their dates of knowledge are different, subsection (5)(*b*) above shall be read as referring to the earliest of those dates.

[11A Actions in respect of defective products

(1) This section shall apply to an action for damages by virtue of any provision of Part I of the Consumer Protection Act 1987.

(2) None of the time limits given in the preceding provisions of this Act shall apply to an action to which this section applies.

(3) An action to which this section applies shall not be brought after the expiration of the period of ten years from the relevant time, within the meaning of section 4 of the said Act of 1987; and this subsection shall operate to extinguish a right of action and shall do so whether or not that right of action had accrued, or time under the following provisions of this Act had begun to run, at the end of the said period of ten years.

(4) Subject to subsection (5) below, an action to which this section applies in which the damages claimed by the plaintiff consist of or include damages in respect of personal injuries to the plaintiff or any other person or loss of or damage to any property, shall not be brought after the expiration of the period of three years from whichever is the later of—

(*a*) the date on which the cause of action accrued; and
(*b*) the date of knowledge of the injured person or, in the case of loss of or damage to property, the date of knowledge of the plaintiff or (if earlier) of any person in whom his cause of action was previously vested.

(5) If in a case where the damages claimed by the plaintiff consist of or include damages in respect of personal injuries to the plaintiff or any other person the injured person died before the expiration of the period mentioned in subsection (4) above, that subsection shall have effect as respects the cause of action surviving for the benefit of his estate by virtue of section 1 of the Law Reform (Miscellaneous Provisions) Act 1934 as if for the reference to that period there were substituted a reference to the period of three years from whichever is the later of—

(*a*) the date of death; and
(*b*) the date of the personal representative's knowledge.

(6) For the purposes of this section "personal representative" includes any person who is or has been a personal representative of the deceased, including an executor who has not proved the will (whether or not he has renounced probate) but not anyone appointed only as a special personal representative in relation to settled land; and regard shall be had to any knowledge acquired by any such person while a personal representative or previously.

(7) If there is more than one personal representative and their dates of knowledge are different, subsection (5)(*b*) above shall be read as referring to the earliest of those dates.

(8) Expressions used in this section or section 14 of this Act and in Part I of the Consumer Protection Act 1987 have the same meanings in this section or that section as in that Part; and section 1(1) of that Act (Part I to be construed as enacted for the purpose of complying with the product liability Directive) shall apply for the purpose of construing this section and the following provisions of this Act so far as they relate to an action by virtue of any provisions of that Part as it applies for the purpose of construing that Part.][1]

[1] Inserted by the Consumer Protection Act 1987, ss 6(6), 50(2), 1 Sch 1.

12 Special time limit for actions under Fatal Accidents legislation

(1) An action under the Fatal Accidents Act 1976 shall not be brought if the death occurred when the person injured could no longer maintain an action and recover damages in respect of the injury (whether because of a time limit in this Act or in any other Act, or for any other reason).

Where any such action by the injured person would have been barred by the time limit in section 11 [or 11A][1] of this Act, no account shall be taken of the possibility of that time limit being overridden under section 33 of this Act.

(2) None of the time limits given in the preceding provisions of this Act shall apply to an action under the Fatal Accidents Act 1976, but no such action shall be brought after the expiration of three years from—

(*a*) the date of death; or
(*b*) the date of knowledge of the person for whose benefit the action is brought;

whichever is the later.

(3) An action under the Fatal Accidents Act 1976 shall be one to which sections 28, 33 and 35 of this Act apply, and the application to any such action of the time limit under subsection (2) above shall be subject to section 39; but otherwise Parts II and III of this Act shall not apply to any such action.

---

1 Inserted by the Consumer Protection Act 1987, ss 6(6), 50(2), 1 Sch 2.

---

13 Operation of time limit under section 12 in relation to different dependants

(1) Where there is more than one person for whose benefit an action under the Fatal Accidents Act 1976 is brought, section 12(2)(*b*) of this Act shall be applied separately to each of them.

(2) Subject to subsection (3) below, if by virtue of subsection (1) above the action would be outside the time limit given by section 12(2) as regards one or more, but not all, of the persons for whose benefit it is brought, the court shall direct that any person as regards whom the action would be outside that limit shall be excluded from those for whom the action is brought.

(3) The court shall not give such a direction if it is shown that if the action were brought exclusively for the benefit of the person in question it would not be defeated by a defence of limitation (whether in consequence of section 28 of this Act or an agreement between the parties not to raise the defence, or otherwise).

14 Definition of date of knowledge for purposes of sections 11 and 12

(1) [Subject to subsection (1A) below,][1] in sections 11 and 12 of this Act references to a person's date of knowledge are references to the date on which he first had knowledge of the following facts—

(*a*) that the injury in question was significant; and
(*b*) that the injury was attributable in whole or in part to the act or omission which is alleged to constitute negligence, nuisance or breach of duty; and
(*c*) the identity of the defendant; and
(*d*) if it is alleged that the act or omission was that of a person other than the defendant, the identity of that person and the additional facts supporting the bringing of an action against the defendant;

and knowledge that any acts or omissions did or did not, as a matter of law, involve negligence, nuisance or breach of duty is irrelevant.

[(1A) In section 11A of this Act and in section 12 of this Act so far as that section applies to an action by virtue of section 6(1)(*a*) of the Consumer Protection Act 1987 (death caused by defective product) references to a person's date of knowledge are references to the date on which he first had knowledge of the following facts—

(*a*) such facts about the damage caused by the defect as would lead a reasonable person who had suffered such damage to consider it sufficiently serious to justify his instituting proceedings for damages against a defendant who did not dispute liability and was able to satisfy a judgment; and
(*b*) that the damage was wholly or partly attributable to the facts and circumstances alleged to constitute the defect; and
(*c*) the identity of the defendant;

but, in determining the date on which a person first had such knowledge there shall be disregarded both the extent (if any) of that person's knowledge on any date of whether particular facts or circumstances would or would not, as a matter of law, constitute a defect and, in a case relating to loss of or damage to property, any knowledge which that person had on a date on which he had no right of action by virtue of Part I of that Act in respect of the loss or damage.][1]

(2) For the purposes of this section an injury is significant if the person whose date of knowledge is in question would reasonably have considered it sufficiently serious to justify his instituting proceedings for damages against a defendant who did not dispute liability and was able to satisfy a judgment.

(3) For the purposes of this section a person's knowledge includes knowledge which he might reasonably have been expected to acquire—

(*a*) from facts observable or ascertainable by him; or
(*b*) from facts ascertainable by him with the help of medical or other appropriate expert advice which it is reasonable for him to seek;

but a person shall not be fixed under this subsection with knowledge of a fact ascertainable only with the help of expert advice so long as he has taken all reasonable steps to obtain (and, where appropriate, to act on) that advice.

---

1 Inserted by the Consumer Protection Act 1987, ss 6(6), 50(2), 1 Sch 3.

[*Actions in respect of latent damage not involving personal injuries*

14A Special time limit for negligence actions where facts relevant to cause of action are not known at date of accrual

(1) This section applies to any action for damages for negligence, other than one to which section 11 of this Act applies, where the starting date for reckoning the period of limitation under subsection (4)(*b*) below falls after the date on which the cause of action accrued.

(2) Section 2 of this Act shall not apply to an action to which this section applies.

(3) An action to which this section applies shall not be brought after the expiration of the period applicable in accordance with subsection (4) below.

(4) That period is either—

(*a*) six years from the date on which the cause of action accrued; or
(*b*) three years from the starting date as defined by subsection (5) below, if that period expires later than the period mentioned in paragraph (*a*) above.

(5) For the purposes of this section, the starting date for reckoning the period of limitation under subsection (4)(*b*) above is the earliest date on which the plaintiff or any person in whom the cause of action was vested before him first had both the knowledge required for bringing an action for damages in respect of the relevant damage and a right to bring such an action.

(6) In subsection (5) above "the knowledge required for bringing an action for damages in respect of the relevant damage" means knowledge both—

(*a*) of the material facts about the damage in respect of which damages are claimed; and

(*b*) of the other facts relevant to the current action mentioned in subsection (8) below.

(7) For the purposes of subsection (6)(*a*) above, the material facts about the damage are such facts about the damage as would lead a reasonable person who had suffered such damage to consider it sufficiently serious to justify his instituting proceedings for damages against a defendant who did not dispute liability and was able to satisfy a judgment.

(8) The other facts referred to in subsection (6)(*b*) above are—

(*a*) that the damage was attributable in whole or in part to the act or omission which is alleged to constitute negligence; and

(*b*) the identity of the defendant; and

(*c*) if it is alleged that the act or omission was that of a person other than the defendant, the identity of that person and the additional facts supporting the bringing of an action against the defendant.

(9) Knowledge that any acts or omissions did or did not, as a matter of law, involve negligence is irrelevant for the purposes of subsection (5) above.

(10) For the purposes of this section a person's knowledge includes knowledge which he might reasonably have been expected to acquire—

(*a*) from facts observable or ascertainable by him; or

(*b*) from facts ascertainable by him with the help of appropriate expert advice which it is reasonable for him to seek;

but a person shall not be taken by virtue of this subsection to have knowledge of a fact ascertainable only with the help of expert advice so long as he has taken all reasonable steps to obtain (and, where appropriate, to act on) that advice.][1]

---

1 Inserted with saving by the Latent Damage Act 1986, ss 1, 4 (1)(2).

[14B Overriding time limit for negligence actions not involving personal injuries

(1) An action for damages for negligence, other than one to which section 11 of this Act applies, shall not be brought after the expiration of fifteen years from the date (or, if more than one, from the last of the dates) on which there occurred any act or omission—

(*a*) which is alleged to constitute negligence; and

(*b*) to which the damage in respect of which damages are claimed is alleged to be attributable (in whole or in part).

(2) This section bars the right of action in a case to which subsection (1) above applies notwithstanding that—

(*a*) the cause of action has not yet accrued; or

(*b*) where section 14A of this Act applies to the action, the date which is for the purposes of that section the starting date for reckoning the period mentioned in subsection (4)(*b*) of that section has not yet occurred;

before the end of the period of limitation prescribed by this section.][1]

---

[1] Inserted with saving by the Latent Damage Act 1986, ss 1, 4(1)(2).

Actions to recover land and rent

15 Time limit for actions to recover land

(1) No action shall be brought by any person to recover any land after the expiration of twelve years from the date on which the right of action accrued to him or, if it first accrued to some person through whom he claims, to that person.

(2) Subject to the following provisions of this section, where—

(*a*) the estate or interest claimed was an estate or interest in reversion or remainder or any other future estate or interest and the right of action to recover the land accrued on the date on which the estate or interest fell into possession by the determination of the preceding estate or interest; and

(*b*) the person entitled to the preceding estate or interest (not being a term of years absolute) was not in possession of the land on that date;

no action shall be brought by the person entitled to the succeeding estate or interest after the expiration of twelve years from the date on which the right of action accrued to the person entitled to the preceding estate or interest or six years from the date on which the right of action accrued to the person entitled to the succeeding estate or interest, whichever period last expires.

(3) Subsection (2) above shall not apply to any estate or interest which falls into possession on the determination of an entailed interest and which might have been barred by the person entitled to the entailed interest.

(4) No person shall bring an action to recover any estate or interest in land under an assurance taking effect after the right of action to recover the land had accrued to the person by whom the assurance was made or some person through whom he claimed or some person entitled to a preceding estate or interest, unless the action is brought within the period during which the person by whom the assurance was made could have brought such an action.

(5) Where any person is entitled to any estate or interest in land in possession and, while so entitled, is also entitled to any future estate or interest in that land, and his right to recover the estate or interest in possession is barred under this Act, no action shall be brought by that person, or by any person claiming through him, in respect of the future estate or interest, unless in the meantime possession of the land has been recovered by a person entitled to an intermediate estate or interest.

(6) Part I of Schedule 1 to this Act contains provisions for determining the date of accrual of rights of action to recover land in the cases there mentioned.

(7) Part II of that Schedule contains provisions modifying the provisions of this section in their application to actions brought by, or by a person claiming through, the Crown or any spiritual or eleemosynary corporation sole.

16 Time limit for redemption actions

When a mortgagee of land has been in possession of any of the mortgaged land for a period of twelve years, no action to redeem the land of which the mortgagee has been so in possession shall be brought after the end of that period by the mortgagor or any person claiming through him.

17 Extinction of title to land after expiration of time limit

Subject to—

(*a*) section 18 of this Act; and
(*b*) section 75 of the Land Registration Act 1925;

at the expiration of the period prescribed by this Act for any person to bring an action to recover land (including a redemption action) the title of that person to the land shall be extinguished.

18 Settled land and land held on trust

(1) Subject to section 21(1) and (2) of this Act, the provisions of this Act shall apply to equitable interests in land, including interests in the proceeds of the sale of land held upon trust for sale, as they apply to legal estates.

Accordingly a right of action to recover the land shall, for the purposes of this Act but not otherwise, be treated as accruing to a person entitled in possession to such an equitable interest in the like manner and circumstances, and on the same date, as it would accrue if his interest were a legal estate in the land (and any relevant provision of Part I of Schedule 1 to this Act shall apply in any such case accordingly).

(2) Where the period prescribed by this Act has expired for the bringing of an action to recover land by a tenant for life or a statutory owner of settled land—

(*a*) his legal estate shall not be extinguished if and so long as the right of action to recover the land of any person entitled to a beneficial interest in the land either has not accrued or has not been barred by this Act; and
(*b*) the legal estate shall accordingly remain vested in the tenant for life or statutory owner and shall devolve in accordance with the Settled Land Act 1925;

but if and when every such right of action has been barred by this Act, his legal estate shall be extinguished.

(3) Where any land is held upon trust (including a trust for sale) and the period prescribed by this Act has expired for the bringing of an action to recover the land by the trustees, the estate of the trustees shall not be extinguished if and so long as the right of action to recover the land of any person entitled to a beneficial interest in the land or in the proceeds of sale either has not accrued or has not been barred by this Act; but if and when every such right of action has been so barred the estate of the trustees shall be extinguished.

(4) Where—

(*a*) any settled land is vested in a statutory owner; or
(*b*) any land is held upon trust (including a trust for sale);

an action to recover the land may be brought by the statutory owner or trustees on behalf of any person entitled to a beneficial interest in possession in the land or in the proceeds of sale whose right of action has not been barred by this Act, notwithstanding that the right of action of the statutory owner or trustees would apart from this provision have been barred by this Act.

19 Time limit for actions to recover rent

No action shall be brought, or distress made, to recover arrears of rent, or damages in respect of arrears of rent, after the expiration of six years from the date on which the arrears became due.

Actions to recover money secured by a mortgage or charge or to recover proceeds of the sale of land

20 Time limit for actions to recover money secured by a mortgage or charge or to recover proceeds of the sale of land

(1) No action shall be brought to recover—

(*a*) any principal sum of money secured by a mortgage or other charge on property (whether real or personal); or
(*b*) proceeds of the sale of land;

after the expiration of twelve years from the date on which the right to receive the money accrued.

(2) No foreclosure action in respect of mortgaged personal property shall be brought after the expiration of twelve years from the date on which the right to foreclose accrued.

But if the mortgagee was in possession of the mortgaged property after that date, the right to foreclose on the property which was in his possession shall not be treated as having accrued for the purposes of this subsection until the date on which his possession discontinued.

(3) The right to receive any principal sum of money secured by a mortgage or other charge and the right to foreclose on the property subject to the mortgage or charge shall not be treated as accruing so long as that property comprises any future interest or any life insurance policy which has not matured or been determined.

(4) Nothing in this section shall apply to a foreclosure action in respect of mortgaged land, but the provisions of this Act relating to actions to recover land shall apply to such an action.

(5) Subject to subsections (6) and (7) below, no action to recover arrears of interest payable in respect of any sum of money secured by a mortgage or other charge or payable in respect of proceeds of the sale of land, or to recover damages in respect of such arrears shall be brought after the expiration of six years from the date on which the interest became due.

(6) Where—

(*a*) a prior mortgagee or other incumbrancer has been in possession of the property charged; and
(*b*) an action is brought within one year of the discontinuance of that possession by the subsequent incumbrancer;

the subsequent incumbrancer may recover by that action all the arrears of interest which fell due during the period of possession by the prior incumbrancer or damages in respect of those arrears, notwithstanding that the period exceeded six years.

(7) Where—

(*a*) the property subject to the mortgage or charge comprises any future interest or life insurance policy; and

(*b*) it is a term of the mortgage or charge that arrears of interest shall be treated as part of the principal sum of money secured by the mortgage or charge;

interest shall not be treated as becoming due before the right to recover the principal sum of money has accrued or is treated as having accrued.

Actions in respect of trust property or the personal estate of deceased persons

21 Time limit for actions in respect of trust property

(1) No period of limitation prescribed by this Act shall apply to an action by a beneficiary under a trust, being an action—

(*a*) in respect of any fraud or fraudulent breach of trust to which the trustee was a party or privy; or

(*b*) to recover from the trustee trust property or the proceeds of trust property in the possession of the trustee, or previously received by the trustee and converted to his use.

(2) Where a trustee who is also a beneficiary under the trust receives or retains trust property or its proceeds as his share on a distribution of trust property under the trust, his liability in any action brought by virtue of subsection (1)(*b*) above to recover that property or its proceeds after the expiration of the period of limitation prescribed by this Act for bringing an action to recover trust property shall be limited to the excess over his proper share.

This subsection only applies if the trustee acted honestly and reasonably in making the distribution.

(3) Subject to the preceding provisions of this section, an action by a beneficiary to recover trust property or in respect of any breach of trust, not being an action for which a period of limitation is prescribed by any other provision of this Act, shall not be brought after the expiration of six years from the date on which the right of action accrued.

For the purposes of this subsection, the right of action shall not be treated as having accrued to any beneficiary entitled to a future interest in the trust property until the interest fell into possession.

(4) No beneficiary as against whom there would be a good defence under this Act shall derive any greater or other benefit from a judgment or order obtained by any other beneficiary than he could have obtained if he had brought the action and this Act had been pleaded in defence.

22 Time limit for actions claiming personal estate of a deceased person

Subject to section 21(1) and (2) of this Act—

(*a*) no action in respect of any claim to the personal estate of a deceased person or to any share or interest in any such estate (whether under a will or on intestacy) shall be brought after the expiration of twelve years from the date on which the right to receive the share or interest accrued; and

(*b*) no action to recover arrears of interest in respect of any legacy, or damages in respect of such arrears, shall be brought after the expiration of six years from the date on which the interest became due.

Actions for an account

23 Time limit in respect of actions for an account

An action for an account shall not be brought after the expiration of any time limit under this Act which is applicable to the claim which is the basis of the duty to account.

Miscellaneous and supplemental

24 Time limit for actions to enforce judgments

(1) An action shall not be brought upon any judgment after the expiration of six years from the date on which the judgment became enforceable.

(2) No arrears of interest in respect of any judgment debt shall be recovered after the expiration of six years from the date on which the interest became due.

25 Time limit for actions to enforce advowsons and extinction of title to advowsons

[Repealed by the Patronage (Benefices) Measure 1986].

26 Administration to date back to death

For the purposes of the provisions of this Act relating to actions for the recovery of land and advowsons an administrator of the estate of a deceased person shall be treated as claiming as if there had been no interval of time between the death of the deceased person and the grant of the letters of administration.

27 Cure of defective disentailing assurance

(1) This section applies where—

(*a*) a person entitled in remainder to an entailed interest in any land makes an assurance of his interest which fails to bar the issue in tail or the estates and interests taking effect on the determination of the entailed interest, or fails to bar those estates and interests only; and

(*b*) any person takes possession of the land by virtue of the assurance.

(2) If the person taking possession of the land by virtue of the assurance, or any other person whatsoever (other than a person entitled to possession by virtue of the settlement) is in possession of the land for a period of twelve years from the commencement of the time when the assurance could have operated as an effective bar, the assurance shall thereupon operate, and be treated as having always operated, to bar the issue in tail and the estates and interests taking effect on the determination of the entailed interest.

(3) The reference in subsection (2) above to the time when the assurance could have operated as an effective bar is a reference to the time at which the assurance, as it had then been executed by the person entitled to the entailed interest, would have operated, without the consent of any other person, to bar

the issue in tail and the estates and interests taking effect on the determination of the entailed interest.

PART II

EXTENSION OR EXCLUSION OF ORDINARY TIME LIMITS

Disability

28 Extension of limitation period in case of disability

(1) Subject to the following provisions of this section, if on the date when any right of action accrued for which a period of limitation is prescribed by this Act, the person to whom it accrued was under a disability, the action may be brought at any time before the expiration of six years from the date when he ceased to be under a disability or died (whichever first occurred) notwithstanding that the period of limitation has expired.

(2) This section shall not affect any case where the right of action first accrued to some person (not under a disability) through whom the person under a disability claims.

(3) When a right of action which has accrued to a person under a disability accrues, on the death of that person while still under a disability, to another person under a disability, no further extension of time shall be allowed by reason of the disability of the second person.

(4) No action to recover land or money charged on land shall be brought by virtue of this section by any person after the expiration of thirty years from the date on which the right of action accrued to that person or some person through whom he claims.

[(4A) If the action is one to which section 4A of this Act applies, subsection (1) above shall have effect as if for the words from "at any time" to "occurred)" there were substituted the words "by him at any time before the expiration of three years from the date when he ceased to be under a disability".][1]

(5) If the action is one to which section 10 of this Act applies, subsection (1) above shall have effect as if for the words "six years" there were substituted the words "two years".

(6) If the action is one to which section 11 or 12(2) of this Act applies, subsection (1) above shall have effect as if for the words "six years" there were substituted the words "three years".

[(7) If the action is one to which section 11A of this Act applies or one by virtue of section 6(1)(*a*) of the Consumer Protection Act 1987 (death caused by defective product), subsection (1) above—

(*a*) shall not apply to the time limit prescribed by subsection (3) of the said section 11A or to that time limit as applied by virtue of section 12(1) of this Act; and

(*b*) in relation to any other time limit prescribed by this Act shall have effect as if for the words "six years" there were substituted the words "three years".][2]

1 Inserted by the Administration of Justice Act 1985, ss 57(3), 69(5), 9 Sch 14.

2 Inserted by the Consumer Protection Act 1987, ss 6(6), 50(2), 1 Sch 4.

Notes

(a) Section 28 excluded by the Latent Damage Act 1986, ss 3(3), 4.

(b) Section 28(1) extended with modification by the Merchant Shipping (Liner Conferences) Act 1982, s 8(2)(a).

[28A Extension for cases where the limitation period is the period under section 14A(4)(*b*)

(1) Subject to subsection (2) below, if in the case of any action for which a period of limitation is prescribed by section 14A of this Act—

(*a*) the period applicable in accordance with subsection (4) of that section is the period mentioned in paragraph (*b*) of that subsection;
(*b*) on the date which is for the purposes of that section the starting date for reckoning that period the person by reference to whose knowledge that date fell to be determined under subsection (5) of that section was under a disability; and
(*c*) section 28 of this Act does not apply to the action;

the action may be brought at any time before the expiration of three years from the date when he ceased to be under a disability or died (whichever first occurred) notwithstanding that the period mentioned above has expired.

(2) An action may not be brought by virtue of subsection (1) above after the end of the period of limitation prescribed by section 14B of this Act.][1]

1 Inserted with saving by the Latent Damage Act 1986, ss 2(1), 4(1)(2).

Acknowledgment and part payment

29 Fresh accrual of action on acknowledgment or part payment

(1) Subsections (2) and (3) below apply where any right of action (including a foreclosure action) to recover land or an advowson or any right of a mortgagee of personal property to bring a foreclosure action in respect of the property has accrued.

(2) If the person in possession of the land, benefice or personal property in question acknowledges the title of the person to whom the right of action has accrued—

(*a*) the right shall be treated as having accrued on and not before the date of the acknowledgment; and
(*b*) in the case of a right of action to recover land which has accrued to a person entitled to an estate or interest taking effect on the determination of an entailed interest against whom time is running under section 27 of this Act, section 27 shall thereupon cease to apply to the land.

(3) In the case of a foreclosure or other action by a mortgagee, if the person in possession of the land, benefice or personal property in question or the person liable for the mortgage debt makes any payment in respect of the debt (whether

of principal or interest) the right shall be treated as having accrued on and not before the date of the payment.

(4) Where a mortgagee is by virtue of the mortgage in possession of any mortgaged land and either—

(*a*) receives any sum in respect of the principal or interest of the mortgage debt; or
(*b*) acknowledges the title of the mortgagor, or his equity of redemption;

an action to redeem the land in his possession may be brought at any time before the expiration of twelve years from the date of the payment or acknowledgment.

(5) Subject to subsection (6) below, where any right of action has accrued to recover—

(*a*) any debt or other liquidated pecuniary claim; or
(*b*) any claim to the personal estate of a deceased person or to any share or interest in any such estate;

and the person liable or accountable for the claim acknowledges the claim or makes any payment in respect of it the right shall be treated as having accrued on and not before the date of the acknowledgment or payment.

(6) A payment of a part of the rent or interest due at any time shall not extend the period for claiming the remainder then due, but any payment of interest shall be treated as a payment in respect of the principal debt.

(7) Subject to subsection (6) above, a current period of limitation may be repeatedly extended under this section by further acknowledgments or payments, but a right of action, once barred by this Act, shall not be revived by any subsequent acknowledgment or payment.

30 Formal provisions as to acknowledgments and part payments

(1) To be effective for the purposes of section 29 of this Act, an acknowledgment must be in writing and signed by the person making it.

(2) For the purposes of section 29, any acknowledgment or payment—

(*a*) may be sent by the agent of the person by whom it is required to be made under that section; and
(*b*) shall be made to the person, or to an agent of the person, whose title or claim is being acknowledged or, as the case may be, in respect of whose claim the payment is being made.

31 Effect of acknowledgment or part payment on persons other than the maker or recipient

(1) An acknowledgment of the title to any land, benefice, or mortgaged personalty by any person in possession of it shall bind all other persons in possession during the ensuing period of limitation.

(2) A payment in respect of a mortgage debt by the mortgagor or any other person liable for the debt, or by any person in possession of the mortgaged property, shall, so far as any right of the mortgagee to foreclose or otherwise to recover the property is concerned, bind all other persons in possession of the mortgaged property during the ensuing period of limitation.

(3) Where two or more mortgagees are by virtue of the mortgage in possession of the mortgaged land, an acknowledgment of the mortgagor's title or of his equity of redemption by one of the mortgagees shall only bind him and his successors and shall not bind any other mortgagee or his successors.

(4) Where in a case within subsection (3) above the mortgagee by whom the acknowledgment is given is entitled to a part of the mortgaged land and not to any ascertained part of the mortgage debt the mortgagor shall be entitled to redeem that part of the land on payment, with interest, of the part of the mortgage debt which bears the same proportion to the whole of the debt as the value of the part of the land bears to the whole of the mortgaged land.

(5) Where there are two or more mortgagors, and the title or equity of redemption of one of the mortgagors is acknowledged as mentioned above in this section, the acknowledgment shall be treated as having been made to all the mortgagors.

(6) An acknowledgment of any debt or other liquidated pecuniary claim shall bind the acknowledgor and his successors but not any other person.

(7) A payment made in respect of any debt or other liquidated pecuniary claim shall bind all persons liable in respect of the debt or claim.

(8) An acknowledgment by one of several personal representatives of any claim to the personal estate of a deceased person or to any share or interest in any such estate, or a payment by one of several personal representatives in respect of any such claim, shall bind the estate of the deceased person.

(9) In this section "successor", in relation to any mortgagee or person liable in respect of any debt or claim, means his personal representatives and any other person on whom the rights under the mortgage or, as the case may be, the liability in respect of the debt or claim devolve (whether on death or bankruptcy or the disposition of property or the determination of a limited estate or interest in settled property or otherwise).

Fraud, concealment and mistake

32 Postponement of limitation period in case of fraud, concealment or mistake

(1) Subject to [subsections (3) and (4A)][1] below, where in the case of any action for which a period of limitation is prescribed by this Act, either—

(*a*) the action is based upon the fraud of the defendant; or
(*b*) any fact relevant to the plaintiff's right of action has been deliberately concealed from him by the defendant; or
(*c*) the action is for relief from the consequences of a mistake;

the period of limitation shall not begin to run until the plaintiff has discovered the fraud, concealment or mistake (as the case may be) or could with reasonable diligence have discovered it.

References in this subsection to the defendant include references to the defendant's agent and to any person through whom the defendant claims and his agent.

(2) For the purposes of subsection (1) above, deliberate commission of a breach of duty in circumstances in which it is unlikely to be discovered for some

time amounts to deliberate concealment of the facts involved in that breach of duty.

(3) Nothing in this section shall enable any action—

(*a*) to recover, or recover the value of, any property; or
(*b*) to enforce any charge against, or set aside any transaction affecting, any property;

to be brought against the purchaser of the property or any person claiming through him in any case where the property has been purchased for valuable consideration by an innocent third party since the fraud or concealment or (as the case may be) the transaction in which the mistake was made took place.

(4) A purchaser is an innocent third party for the purposes of this section—

(*a*) in the case of fraud or concealment of any fact relevant to the plaintiff's right of action, if he was not a party to the fraud or (as the case may be) to the concealment of that fact and did not at the time of the purchase know or have reason to believe that the fraud or concealment had taken place; and
(*b*) in the case of mistake, if he did not at the time of the purchase know or have reason to believe that the mistake had been made.

[(4A) Subsection (1) above shall not apply in relation to the time limit prescribed by section 11A(3) of this Act or in relation to that time limit as applied by virtue of section 12(1) of this Act.][2]

[(5) Sections 14A and 14B of this Act shall not apply to any action to which subsection (1)(*b*) above applies (and accordingly the period of limitation referred to in that subsection, in any case to which either of those sections would otherwise apply, is the period applicable under section 2 of this Act).][3]

1 Substituted by the Consumer Protection Act 1987, ss 6(6), 50(2), 1 Sch 5(a). Previously 'subsection (3)'.

2 Inserted by the Consumer Protection Act 1987, ss 6(6), 50(2), 1 Sch 5(b).

3 Added with saving by Latent Damage Act 1986, ss 2(2), 4(1)(2).

Notes
(a) Section 32(1) was extended by the Merchant Shipping (Liner Conferences) Act 1982, s 8(2)(b).

[*Discretionary extension of time limit for actions for libel or slander*

32A Discretionary extension of time limit for actions for libel or slander

Where a person to whom a cause of action for libel or slander has accrued has not brought such an action within the period of three years mentioned in section 4A of this Act (or, where applicable, the period allowed by section 28(1) as modified by section 28(4A)) because all or any of the facts relevant to that cause of action did not become known to him until after the expiration of that period, such an action—

(*a*) may be brought by him at any time before the expiration of one year from the earliest date on which he knew all the facts relevant to that cause of action; but
(*b*) shall not be brought without the leave of the High Court.][1]

1 Inserted by the Administration of Justice Act 1985, ss 57(4), 69(5), 9 Sch 14.

Discretionary exclusion of time limit for actions in respect of personal injuries or death

33 Discretionary exclusion of time limit for actions in respect of personal injuries or death

(1) If it appears to the court that it would be equitable to allow an action to proceed having regard to the degree to which—

(*a*) the provisions of section 11 [or 11A][1] or 12 of this Act prejudice the plaintiff or any person whom he represents; and
(*b*) any decision of the court under this subsection would prejudice the defendant or any person whom he represents;

the court may direct that those provisions shall not apply to the action, or shall not apply to any specified cause of action to which the action relates.

[(1A) The court shall not under this section disapply—

(*a*) subsection (3) of section 11A; or
(*b*) where the damages claimed by the plaintiff are confined to damages for loss of or damage to any property, any other provision in its application to an action by virtue of Part I of the Consumer Protection Act 1987.][2]

(2) The court shall not under this section disapply section 12(1) except where the reason why the person injured could no longer maintain an action was because of the time limit in section 11 [or subsection (4) of section 11A].[3]

If, for example, the person injured could at his death no longer maintain an action under the Fatal Accidents Act 1976 because of the time limit in Article 29 in Schedule 1 to the Carriage by Air Act 1961, the court has no power to direct that section 12(1) shall not apply.

(3) In acting under this section the court shall have regard to all the circumstances of the case and in particular to—

(*a*) the length of, and the reasons for, the delay on the part of the plaintiff;
(*b*) the extent to which, having regard to the delay, the evidence adduced or likely to be adduced by the plaintiff or the defendant is or is likely to be less cogent than if the action had been brought within the time allowed by section 11 [, by section 11A][4] or (as the case may be) by section 12;
(*c*) the conduct of the defendant after the case of action arose, including the extent (if any) to which he responded to requests reasonably made by the plaintiff for information or inspection for the purpose of ascertaining facts which were or might be relevant to the plaintiff's cause of action against the defendant;
(*d*) the duration of any disability of the plaintiff arising after the date of the accrual of the cause of action;
(*e*) the extent to which the plaintiff acted promptly and reasonably once he knew whether or not the act or omission of the defendant, to which the injury was attributable, might be capable at the time of giving rise to an action for damages;
(*f*) the steps, if any, taken by the plaintiff to obtain medical, legal or other expert advice and the nature of any such advice he may have received.

(4) In a case where the person injured died when, because of section 11 [or subsection (4) of section 11A][3], he could no longer maintain an action and recover damages in respect of the injury, the court shall have regard in particular to the length of, and the reasons for, the delay on the part of the deceased.

(5) In a case under subsection (4) above, or any other case where the time limit, or one of the time limits, depends on the date of knowledge of a person other than the plaintiff, subsection (3) above shall have effect with appropriate modifications, and shall have effect in particular as if references to the plaintiff included references to any person whose date of knowledge is or was relevant in determining a time limit.

(6) A direction by the court disapplying the provisions of section 12(1) shall operate to disapply the provisions to the same effect in section 1(1) of the Fatal Accidents Act 1976.

(7) In this section "the court" means the court in which the action has been brought.

(8) References in this section to section 11 [or 11A][5] include references to that section as extended by any of the preceding provisions of this Part of this Act or by any provision of Part III of this Act.

---

1 Inserted by the Consumer Protection Act 1987, ss 6(6), 50(2), 1 Sch 6(a).

2 Inserted by the Consumer Protection Act 1987, ss 6(6), 50(2), 1 Sch 6(b).

3 Inserted by the Consumer Protection Act 1987, ss 6(6), 50(2), 1 Sch 6(c).

4 Inserted by the Consumer Protection Act 1987, ss 6(6), 50(2), 1 Sch 6(d).

5 Inserted by the Consumer Protection Act 1987, ss 6(6), 50(2), 1 Sch 6(e).

PART III

MISCELLANEOUS AND GENERAL

34 Application of Act and other limitation enactments to arbitrations

(1) This Act and any other limitation enactment shall apply to arbitrations as they apply to actions in the High Court.

(2) Notwithstanding any term in an arbitration agreement to the effect that no cause of action shall accrue in respect of any matter required by the agreement to be referred until an award is made under the agreement, the cause of action shall, for the purposes of this Act and any other limitation enactment (whether in their application to arbitrations or to other proceedings), be deemed to have accrued in respect of any such matter at the time when it would have accrued but for that term in the agreement.

(3) For the purposes of this Act and of any other limitation enactment an arbitration shall be treated as being commenced—

(*a*) when one party to the arbitration serves on the other party or parties a notice requiring him or them to appoint an arbitrator or to agree to the appointment of an arbitrator; or
(*b*) where the arbitration agreement provides that the reference shall be to a person named or designated in the agreement, when one party to the arbitration serves on the other party or parties a notice requiring him or them to submit the dispute to the person so named or designated.

(4) Any such notice may be served either—

(*a*) by delivering it to the person on whom it is to be served; or
(*b*) by leaving it at the usual or last-known place of abode in England and Wales of that person; or

(*c*) by sending it by post in a registered letter addressed to that person at his usual or last-known place of abode in England and Wales;

as well as in any other manner provided in the arbitration agreement.

(5) Where the High Court—

(*a*) orders that an award be set aside; or
(*b*) orders, after the commencement of an arbitration, that the arbitration agreement shall cease to have effect with respect to the dispute referred;

the court may further order that the period between the commencement of the arbitration and the date of the order of the court shall be excluded in computing the time prescribed by this Act or by any other limitation enactment for the commencement of proceedings (including arbitration) with respect to the dispute referred.

(6) This section shall apply to an arbitration under an Act of Parliament as well as to an arbitration pursuant to an arbitration agreement.

Subsections (3) and (4) above shall have effect, in relation to an arbitration under an Act, as if for the references to the arbitration agreement there were substituted references to such of the provisions of the Act or of any order, scheme, rules, regulations or byelaws made under the Act as relate to the arbitration.

(7) In this section—

(*a*) "arbitration", "arbitration agreement" and "award" have the same meanings as in Part I of the Arbitration Act 1950; and
(*b*) references to any other limitation enactment are references to any other enactment relating to the limitation of actions, whether passed before or after the passing of this Act.

Notes

(a) Section 34 extended by the Foreign Limitation Periods Act 1984, ss 5, 7(3).

(b) Section 34(5) modified by the Foreign Limitation Periods Act 1984, ss 5, 7(3).

---

35 New claims in pending actions: rules of court

(1) For the purposes of this Act, any new claim made in the course of any action shall be deemed to be a separate action and to have been commenced—

(*a*) in the case of a new claim made in or by way of third party proceedings, on the date on which those proceedings were commenced; and
(*b*) in the case of any other new claim, on the same date as the original action.

(2) In this section a new claim means any claim by way of set-off or counterclaim, and any claim involving either—
(*a*) the addition or substitution of a new cause of action; or
(*b*) the addition or substitution of a new party;

and "third party proceedings" means any proceedings brought in the course of any action by any party to the action against a person not previously a party to the action, other than proceedings brought by joining any such person as defendant to any claim already made in the original action by the party bringing the proceedings.

(3) Except as provided by section 33 of this Act or by rules of court, neither the High Court nor any county court shall allow a new claim within subsection (1)(*b*) above, other than an original set-off or counterclaim, to be made in the course of any action after the expiry of any time limit under this Act which would affect a new action to enforce that claim.

For the purposes of this subsection, a claim is an original set-off or an original counterclaim if it is a claim made by way of set-off or (as the case may be) by way of counterclaim by a party who has not previously made any claim in the action.

(4) Rules of court may provide for allowing a new claim to which subsection (3) above applies to be made as there mentioned, but only if the conditions specified in subsection (5) below are satisfied, and subject to any further restrictions the rules may impose.

(5) The conditions referred to in subsection (4) above are the following—

(*a*) in the case of a claim involving a new cause of action, if the new cause of action arises out of the same facts or substantially the same facts as are already in issue on any claim previously made in the original action; and

(*b*) in the case of a claim involving a new party, if the addition or substitution of the new party is necessary for the determination of the original action.

(6) The addition or substitution of a new party shall not be regarded for the purposes of subsection (5)(*b*) above as necessary for the determination of the original action unless either—

(*a*) the new party is substituted for a party whose name was given in any claim made in the original action in mistake for the new party's name; or

(*b*) any claim already made in the original action cannot be maintained by or against an existing party unless the new party is joined or substituted as plaintiff or defendant in that action.

(7) Subject to subsection (4) above, rules of court may provide for allowing a party to any action to claim relief in a new capacity in respect of a new cause of action notwithstanding that he had no title to make that claim at the date of the commencement of the action.

This subsection shall not be taken as prejudicing the power of rules of court to provide for allowing a party to claim relief in a new capacity without adding or substituting a new cause of action.

(8) Subsections (3) to (7) above shall apply in relation to a new claim made in the course of third party proceedings as if those proceedings were the original action, and subject to such other modifications as may be prescribed by rules of court in any case or class of case.

(9) [Repealed by the Supreme Court Act 1981, s 152(4), 7 Sch].

Notes

(a) Section 35 extended by the Merchant Shipping (Liner Conferences) Act 1982, s 8(2)(c) and the Foreign Limitation Periods Act 1984, ss 1, 2, 7(3).

---

36 Equitable jurisdiction and remedies

(1) The following time limits under this Act, that is to say—

(*a*) the time limit under section 2 for actions founded on tort;

[(*aa*) the time limit under section 4A for actions for libel or slander;][1]

(*b*) the time limit under section 5 for actions founded on simple contract;
(*c*) the time limit under section 7 for actions to enforce awards where the submission is not by an instrument under seal;
(*d*) the time limit under section 8 for actions on a specialty;
(*e*) the time limit under section 9 for actions to recover a sum recoverable by virtue of any enactment; and
(*f*) the time limit under section 24 for actions to enforce a judgment;

shall not apply to any claim for specific performance of a contract or for an injunction or for other equitable relief, except in so far as any such time limit may be applied by the court by analogy in like manner as the corresponding time limit under any enactment repealed by the Limitation Act 1939 was applied before 1st July 1940.

(2) Nothing in this Act shall affect any equitable jurisdiction to refuse relief on the ground of acquiescence or otherwise.

---

1 Inserted by the Administration of Justice Act 1985, ss 57(5), 69(5), 9 Sch 14.

---

37 Application to the Crown and the Duke of Cornwall

(1) Except as otherwise expressly provided in this Act, and without prejudice to section 39, this Act shall apply to proceedings by or against the Crown in like manner as it applies to proceedings between subjects.

(2) Notwithstanding subsection (1) above, this Act shall not apply to—
(*a*) any proceedings by the Crown for the recovery of any tax or duty or interest on any tax or duty;
(*b*) any forfeiture proceedings under the customs and excise Acts (within the meaning of the Customs and Excise Management Act 1979); or
(*c*) any proceedings in respect of the forfeiture of a ship.

In this subsection "duty" includes any debt due to Her Majesty under section 16 of the Tithe Act 1936, and "ship" includes every description of vessel used in navigation not propelled by oars.

(3) For the purposes of this section, proceedings by or against the Crown include—

(*a*) proceedings by or against Her Majesty in right of the Duchy of Lancaster;
(*b*) proceedings by or against any Government department or any officer of the Crown as such or any person acting on behalf of the Crown; and
(*c*) proceedings by or against the Duke of Cornwall.

(4) For the purpose of the provisions of this Act relating to actions for the recovery of land and advowsons, references to the Crown shall include references to Her Majesty in right of the Duchy of Lancaster; and those provisions shall apply to lands and advowsons forming part of the possessions of the Duchy of Cornwall as if for the references to the Crown there were substituted references to the Duke of Cornwall as defined in the Duchy of Cornwall Management Act 1863.

(5) For the purposes of this Act a proceeding by petition of right (in any case where any such proceeding lies, by virtue of any saving in section 40 of the Crown Proceedings Act 1947, notwithstanding the general abolition by that Act

of proceedings by way of petition of right) shall be treated as being commenced on the date on which the petition is presented.

(6) Nothing in this Act shall affect the prerogative right of Her Majesty (whether in right of the Crown or the Duchy of Lancaster) or of the Duke of Cornwall to any gold or silver mine.

38 Interpretation

(1) In this Act, unless the context otherwise requires—

"action" includes any proceeding in a court of law, including an ecclesiastical court;

"land" includes corporeal hereditaments, tithes and rentcharges and any legal or equitable estate or interest therein, including an interest in the proceeds of the sale of land held upon trust for sale, but except as provided above in this definition does not include any incorporeal hereditament;

"personal estate" and "personal property" do not include chattels real;

"personal injuries" includes any disease and any impairment of a person's physical or mental condition, and "injury" and cognate expressions shall be construed accordingly;

"rent" includes a rentcharge and a rentservice;

"rentcharge" means any annuity or periodical sum of money charged upon or payable out of land, except a rentservice or interest on a mortgage on land;

"settled land", "statutory owner" and "tenant for life" have the same meanings respectively as in the Settled Land Act 1925;

"trust" and "trustee" have the same meanings respectively as in the Trustee Act 1925; and

"trust for sale" has the same meaning as in the Law of Property Act 1925.

(2) For the purposes of this Act a person shall be treated as under a disability while he is an infant, or of unsound mind.

(3) For the purposes of subsection (2) above a person is of unsound mind if he is a person who, by reason of mental disorder within the meaning of the [Mental Health Act 1983][1], is incapable of managing and administering his property and affairs.

(4) Without prejudice to the generality of subsection (3) above, a person shall be conclusively presumed for the purposes of subsection (2) above to be of unsound mind—

(*a*) while he is liable to be detained or subject to guardianship under [the Mental Health Act 1983 (otherwise than by virtue of section 35 or 89)][2]; and

[(*b*) while he is receiving treatment as an in-patient in any hospital within the meaning of the Mental Health Act 1983 or mental nursing home within the meaning of the Nursing Homes Act 1975 without being liable to be detained under the said Act of 1983 (otherwise than by virtue of section 35 or 89), being treatment which follows without any interval a period during which he was liable to be detained or subject to guardianship under the Mental Health Act 1959, or the said Act of 1983 (otherwise than by virtue of section 35 or 89) or by virtue of any enactment repealed or excluded by the Mental Health Act 1959].[3]

(5) Subject to subsection (6) below, a person shall be treated as claiming through another person if he became entitled by, through, under, or by the act of that other person to the right claimed, and any person whose estate or interest might have been barred by a person entitled to an entailed interest in possession shall be treated as claiming through the person so entitled.

(6) A person becoming entitled to any estate or interest by virtue of a special power of appointment shall not be treated as claiming through the appointor.

(7) References in this Act to a right of action to recover land shall include references to a right to enter into possession of the land or, in the case of rentcharges and tithes, to distrain for arrears of rent or tithe, and references to the bringing of such an action shall include references to the making of such an entry or distress.

(8) References in this Act to the possession of land shall, in the case of tithes and rentcharges, be construed as references to the receipt of the tithe or rent, and references to the date of dispossession or discontinuance of possession of land shall, in the case of rentcharges, be construed as references to the date of the last receipt of rent.

(9) References in Part II of this Act to a right of action shall include references to—

(*a*) a cause of action;
(*b*) a right to receive money secured by a mortgage or charge on any property;
(*c*) a right to recover proceeds of the sale of land; and
(*d*) a right to receive a share of interest in the personal estate of a deceased person.

(10) References in Part II to the date of the accrual of a right of action shall be construed—

(*a*) in the case of an action upon a judgment, as references to the date on which the judgment became enforceable; and
(*b*) in the case of an action to recover arrears of rent or interest, or damages in respect of arrears of rent or interest, as references to the date on which the rent or interest became due.

---

1 Substituted by the Mental Health Act 1983, s 148, 4 Sch 55(a).

2 Substituted by virtue of the Mental Health Act 1983, s 148, 4 Sch 55(b)(i).

3 Substituted by virtue of the Mental Health Act 1983, s 148, 4 Sch 55(b)(ii).

---

39 Saving for other limitation enactments

This Act shall not apply to any action or arbitration for which a period of limitation is prescribed by or under any other enactment (whether passed before or after the passing of this Act) or to any action or arbitration to which the

Crown is a party and for which, if it were between subjects, a period of limitation would be prescribed by or under any such other enactment.

Transitional provisions, amendments and repeals

40 (1) Schedule 2 to this Act, which contains transitional provisions, shall have effect.

(2) The enactments specified in Schedule 3 to this Act shall have effect subject to the amendments specified in that Schedule, being amendments consequential on the provisions of this Act; but the amendment of any enactment by that Schedule shall not be taken as prejudicing the operation of section 17(2) of the Interpretation Act 1978 (effect of repeals).

(3) [Repeals enactments specified in 4 Sch].

41 (1) This Act may be cited as the Limitation Act 1980.

(2) This Act, except section 35, shall come into force on 1st May 1981.

(3) Section 35 of this Act shall come into force on 1st May 1981 to the extent (if any) that the section substituted for section 28 of the Limitation Act 1939 by section 8 of the Limitation Amendment Act 1980 is in force immediately before that date; but otherwise section 35 shall come into force on such day as the Lord Chancellor may by order made by statutory instrument appoint, and different days may be appointed for different purposes of that section (including its application in relation to different courts or proceedings).

(4) The repeal by this Act of section 14(1) of the Limitation Act 1963 and the corresponding saving in paragraph 2 of Schedule 2 to this Act shall extend to Northern Ireland, but otherwise this Act does not extend to Scotland or to Northern Ireland.

Notes

(a) Power of appointment conferred by s 41(3) fully exercised: 1 May 1981 appointed by SI 1981 No 588, art. 2.

SCHEDULE 1

PROVISIONS WITH RESPECT TO ACTIONS TO RECOVER LAND

PART I

ACCRUAL OF RIGHTS OF ACTION TO RECOVER LAND

Accrual of right of action in case of present interests in land

1 Where the person bringing an action to recover land, or some person through whom he claims, has been in possession of the land, and has while entitled to the land been dispossessed or discontinued his possession, the right of action shall be treated as having accrued on the date of the dispossession or discontinuance.

2 Where any person brings an action to recover any land of a deceased person (whether under a will or on intestacy) and the deceased person—

(*a*) was on the date of his death in possession of the land or, in the case of a rentcharge created by will or taking effect upon his death, in possession of the land charged; and
(*b*) was the last person entitled to the land to be in possession of it;

the right of action shall be treated as having accrued on the date of his death.

3 Where any person brings an action to recover land, being an estate or interest in possession assured otherwise than by will to him, or to some person through whom he claims, and—

(*a*) the person making the assurance was on the date when the assurance took effect in possession of the land or, in the case of a rentcharge created by the assurance, in possession of the land charged; and
(*b*) no person has been in possession of the land by virtue of the assurance;

the right of action shall be treated as having accrued on the date when the assurance took effect.

Accrual of right of action in case of future interests

4 The right of action to recover any land shall, in a case where—

(*a*) the estate or interest claimed was an estate or interest in reversion or remainder or any other future estate or interest; and
(*b*) no person has taken possession of the land by virtue of the estate or interest claimed;

be treated as having accrued on the date on which the estate or interest fell into possession by the determination of the preceding estate or interest.

5 (1) Subject to sub-paragraph (2) below, a tenancy from year to year or other period, without a lease in writing, shall for the purposes of this Act be treated as being determined at the expiration of the first year or other period; and accordingly the right of action of the person entitled to the land subject to the tenancy shall be treated as having accrued at the date on which in accordance with this sub-paragraph the tenancy is determined.

(2) Where any rent has subsequently been received in respect of the tenancy, the right of action shall be treated as having accrued on the date of the last receipt of rent.

6 (1) Where—

(*a*) any person is in possession of land by virtue of a lease in writing by which a rent of not less than ten pounds a year is reserved; and
(*b*) the rent is received by some person wrongfully claiming to be entitled to the land in reversion immediately expectant on the determination of the lease; and
(*c*) no rent is subsequently received by the person rightfully so entitled;

the right of action to recover the land of the person rightfully so entitled shall be treated as having accrued on the date when the rent was first received by the person wrongfully claiming to be so entitled and not on the date of the determination of the lease.

(2) Sub-paragraph (1) above shall not apply to any lease granted by the Crown.

7 Accrual of right of action in case of forfeiture or breach of condition

(1) Subject to sub-paragaph (2) below, a right of action to recover land by virtue of a forfeiture or breach of condition shall be treated as having accrued on the date on which the forfeiture was incurred or the condition broken.

(2) If any such right has accrued to a person entitled to an estate or interest in reversion or remainder and the land was not recovered by virtue of that right, the right of action to recover the land shall not be treated as having accrued to that person until his estate or interest fell into possession, as if no such forfeiture or breach of condition had occurred.

8 Right of action not to accrue or continue unless there is adverse possession

(1) No right of action to recover land shall be treated as accruing unless the land is in the possession of some person in whose favour the period of limitation can run (referred to below in this paragraph as "adverse possession"); and where under the preceding provisions of this Schedule any such right of action is treated as accruing on a certain date and no person is in adverse possession on that date, the right of action shall not be treated as accruing unless and until adverse possession is taken of the land.

(2) Where a right of action to recover land has accrued and after its accrual, before the right is barred, the land ceases to be in adverse possession, the right of action shall no longer be treated as having accrued and no fresh right of action shall be treated as accruing unless and until the land is again taken into adverse possession.

(3) For the purposes of this paragraph—

(*a*) possession of any land subject to a rentcharge by a person (other than the person entitled to the rentcharge) who does not pay the rent shall be treated as adverse possession of the rentcharge; and

(*b*) receipt of rent under a lease by a person wrongfully claiming to be entitled to the land in reversion immediately expectant on the determination of the lease shall be treated as adverse possession of the land.

(4) For the purpose of determining whether a person occupying any land is in adverse possession of the land it shall not be assumed by implication of law that his occupation is by permission of the person entitled to the land merely by virtue of the fact that his occupation is not inconsistent with the latter's present or future enjoyment of the land.

This provision shall not be taken as prejudicing a finding to the effect that a person's occupation of any land is by implied permission of the person entitled to the land in any case where such a finding is justified on the actual facts of the case.

9 Possession of beneficiary not adverse to others interested in settled land or land held on trust for sale

Where any settled land or any land held on trust for sale is in the possession of a person entitled to a beneficial interest in the land or in the proceeds of sale (not being a person solely or absolutely entitled to the land or the proceeds), no right of action to recover the land shall be treated for the purposes of this Act as accruing during that possession to any person in whom the land is vested as tenant for life, statutory owner or trustee, or to any other person entitled to a beneficial interest in the land or the proceeds of sale.

PART II

MODIFICATION OF SECTION 15 WHERE CROWN OR CERTAIN CORPORATIONS SOLE ARE INVOLVED

10 Subject to paragraph 11 below, section 15(1) of this Act shall apply to the bringing of an action to recover any land by the Crown or by any spiritual or eleemosynary corporation sole with the substitution for the reference to twelve years of a reference to thirty years.

11 (1) An action to recover foreshore may be brought by the Crown at any time before the expiration of sixty years from the date mentioned in section 15(1) of this Act.

(2) Where any right of action to recover land which has ceased to be foreshore but remains in the ownership of the Crown accrued when the land was foreshore, the action may be brought at any time before the expiration of—

(*a*) sixty years from the date of accrual of the right of action; or
(*b*) thirty years from the date when the land ceased to be foreshore;

whichever period first expires.

(3) In this paragraph "foreshore" means the shore and bed of the sea and of any tidal water, below the line of the medium high tide between the spring tides and the neap tides.

12 Notwithstanding section 15(1) of this Act, where in the case of any action brought by a person other than the Crown or a spiritual or eleemosynary corporation sole the right of action first accrued to the Crown or any such corporation sole through whom the person in question claims, the action may be brought at any time before the expiration of—

(*a*) the period during which the action could have been brought by the Crown or the corporation sole; or
(*b*) twelve years from the date on which the right of action accrued to some person other than the Crown or the corporation sole;

whichever period first expires.

13 Section 15(2) of this Act shall apply in any case where the Crown or a spiritual or eleemosynary corporation sole is entitled to the succeeding estate or interest with the substitution—

(*a*) for the reference to twelve years of a reference to thirty years; and
(*b*) for the reference to six years of a reference to twelve years.

SCHEDULE 2

TRANSITIONAL PROVISIONS

1 Nothing in this Act shall affect the operation of section 4 of the Limitation Act 1963, as it had effect immediately before 1 January 1979 (being the date on which the Civil Liability (Contribution) Act 1978 came into force), in relation to any case where the damage in question occurred before that date.

2 The amendment made by section 14(1) of the Limitation Act 1963 in section 5 of the Limitation (Enemies and War Prisoners) Act 1945 (which provides that section 5 shall have effect as if for the words "in force in Northern Ireland at the date of the passing of this Act" there were substituted the words "for the time being in force in Northern Ireland") shall continue to have effect notwithstanding the repeal by this Act of section 14(1).

3 It is hereby declared that a decision taken at any time by a court to grant, or not to grant, leave under Part I of the Limitation Act 1963 (which, so far as it related to leave, was repealed by the Limitation Act 1975) does not affect the determination of any question in proceedings under any provision of this Act which corresponds to a provision of the Limitation Act 1975, but in such proceedings account may be taken of evidence admitted in proceedings under Part I of the Limitation Act 1963.

4 (1) In section 33(6) of this Act the reference to section 1(1) of the Fatal Accidents Act 1976 shall be construed as including a reference to section 1 of the Fatal Accidents Act 1846.

(2) Any other reference in that section, or in section 12 or 13 of this Act, to the Fatal Accidents Act 1976 shall be construed as including a reference to the Fatal Accidents Act 1846.

5 Notwithstanding anything in section 29(7) of this Act or in the repeals made by this Act, the Limitation Act 1939 shall continue to have effect in relation to any acknowledgment or payment made before the coming into force of section 6 of the Limitation Amendment Act 1980 (which amended section 23 of the Limitation Act 1939 and made certain repeals in sections 23 and 25 of that Act so as to prevent the revival by acknowledgment or part payment of a right of action barred by that Act) as it had effect immediately before section 6 came into force.

6 Section 28 of the Limitation Act 1939 (provisions as to set-off or counterclaim) shall continue to apply (as originally enacted) to any claim by way of set-off or counterclaim made in an action to which section 35 of the Act does not apply, but as if the reference in section 28 to that Act were a reference to this Act; and, in relation to any such action, references in this Act to section 35 of this Act shall be construed as references to section 28 as it applies by virtue of this paragraph.

7 Section 37(2)(*c*) of this Act shall be treated for the purposes of the Hovercraft Act 1968 as if it were contained in an Act passed before that Act.

8 In relation to a lease granted before the coming into force of section 3(2) of the Limitation Amendment Act 1980 (which substituted "ten pounds a year" for "twenty shillings" in section 9(3) of the Limitation Act 1939), paragraph 6(1)(*a*) of Schedule 1 to this Act shall have effect as if for the words "ten pounds a year" there were substituted the words "twenty shillings".

9 (1) Nothing in any provision of this Act shall—

(*a*) enable any action to be brought which was barred by this Act or (as the case may be) by the Limitation Act 1939 before the relevant date; or
(*b*) affect any action or arbitration commenced before that date or the title to any property which is the subject of any such action or arbitration.

(2) In sub-paragraph (1) above "the relevant date" means—

(*a*) in relation to section 35 of this Act, the date on which that section comes into force in relation to actions of the description in question or, if section 8 of the Limitation Amendment Act 1980 (which substituted the provisions reproduced in section 35 for section 28 of the Limitation Act

1939) is in force immediately before 1st May 1981 in relation to actions of that description, the date on which section 8 came into force in relation to actions of that description; and

(*b*) in relation to any other provision of this Act, 1st August 1980 (being the date of coming into force of the remaining provisions of the Limitation Amendment Act 1980, apart from section 8).

SCHEDULE 3

CONSEQUENTIAL AMENDMENTS

1 [Amends the Land Registration Act 1925, s 83(11)].

2 In section 21A of the Administration of Estates Act 1925 (debtor who becomes creditor's executor by representation or administrator to account for debt to estate) the reference in subsection (2) to the Limitation Act 1939 shall be construed as including a reference to this Act.

3 [Amends Limitation (Enemies and War Prisoners) Act 1945, s 2(1)].

4 [Amends Charitable Trusts (Validation) Act 1954, s 3(4)].

5 [Amends Carriage by Air Act 1961, s 5(3)].

6 [Amends Carriage of Goods by Road Act 1965, s 7(2)(*a*)].

7 [Amends Agriculture Act 1967, 3 Sch 7(6)].

8 [Amends Mines and Quarries (Tips) Act 1969, 3 Sch 6(2)].

9 [Amends Law of Property Act 1969, s 25(5)].

10 [Amends Animals Act 1971, s 10].

11 [Amends Deposit of Poisonous Waste Act 1972, s 2(4)].

12 [Substitutes new s 88(4)(*c*) in Control of Pollution Act 1974].

SCHEDULE 4

[Specifies enactments repealed by s 40(3)].

Appendix 2

Latent Damage Act 1986

The Latent Damage Act 1986 is to a large extent incorporated in the amended version of the Limitation Act 1980 (Appendix 1). This Appendix therefore contains only those parts of the Act not found in the 1980 Act.

An Act to amend the law about limitation of actions in relation to actions for damages for negligence not involving personal injuries; and to provide for a person taking an interest in property to have, in certain circumstances, a cause of action in respect of negligent damage to the property occurring before he takes that interest. [18 July 1986]

Time limits for negligence actions in respect of latent damage not involving personal injuries

1 [Amends the Limitation Act 1980 by inserting ss 14A and 14B]

2 [Contains consequential amendments to the Limitation Act 1980]

Accrual of cause of action to successive owners in respect of latent damage to property

3 Accrual of cause of action to successive owners in respect of latent damage to property

(1) Subject to the following provisions of this section, where—

(*a*) a cause of action ("the original cause of action") has accrued to any person in respect of any negligence to which damage to any property in which he has an interest is attributable (in whole or in part); and

(*b*) another person acquires an interest in that property after the date on which the original cause of action accrued but before the material facts about the damage have become known to any person who, at the time when he first has knowledge of those facts, has any interest in the property;

a fresh cause of action in respect of that negligence shall accrue to that other person on the date which he acquires his interest in the property.

(2) A cause of action accruing to any person by virtue of subsection (1) above—

(*a*) shall be treated as if based on breach of a duty of care at common law owed to the person to whom it accrues; and

(*b*) shall be treated for the purposes of section 14A of the 1980 Act (special time limit for negligence actions where facts relevant to cause of action are not known at date of accrual) as having accrued on the date on which the original cause of action accrued.

(3) Section 28 of the 1980 Act (extension of limitation period in case of disability) shall not apply in relation to any such cause of action.

(4) Subsection (1) above shall not apply in any case where the person acquiring an interest in the damaged property is either—

(*a*) a person in whom the original cause of action vests by operation of law; or

(*b*) a person in whom the interest in that property vests by virtue of any order made by a court under section 538 of the Companies Act 1985 (vesting of company property in liquidator).

(5) For the purposes of subsection (1)(*b*) above, the material facts about the damage are such facts about the damage as would lead a reasonable person who has an interest in the damaged property at the time when those facts become known to him to consider it sufficiently serious to justify his instituting proceedings for damages against a defendant who did not dispute liability and was able to satisfy a judgment.

(6) For the purposes of this section a person's knowledge includes knowledge which he might reasonably have been expected to acquire—

(*a*) from facts observable or ascertainable by him; or

(*b*) from facts ascertainable by him with the help of appropriate expert advice which it is reasonable for him to seek;

but a person shall not be taken by virtue of this subsection to have knowledge of a fact ascertainable by him only with the help of expert advice so long as he has taken all reasonable steps to obtain (and, where appropriate, to act on) that advice.

(7) This section shall bind the Crown, but as regards the Crown's liability in tort shall not bind the Crown further than the Crown is made liable in tort by the Crown Proceedings Act 1947.

Supplementary

4 Transitional provisions

(1) Nothing in section 1 or 2 of this Act shall—

(*a*) enable any action to be brought which was barred by the 1980 Act or (as the case may be) by the Limitation Act 1939 before this Act comes into force; or

(*b*) affect any action commenced before this Act comes into force.

(2) Subject to subsection (1) above, sections 1 and 2 of this Act shall have effect in relation to causes of action accruing before, as well as in relation to causes of action accruing after, this Act comes into force.

(3) Section 3 of this Act shall only apply in cases where an interest in damaged property is acquired after this Act comes into force but shall so apply, subject to subsection (4) below, irrespective of whether the original cause of action accrued before or after this Act comes into force.

(4) Where—

(*a*) a person acquires an interest in damaged property in circumstances to which section 3 would apart from this subsection apply; but

(*b*) the original cause of action accrued more than six years before this Act comes into force;

a cause of action shall not accrue to that person by virtue of subsection (1) of that section unless section 32(1)(*b*) of the 1980 Act (postponement of limitation period in case of deliberate concealment of relevant facts) would apply to any action founded on the original cause of action.

5 Citation, interpretation, commencement and extent

(1) This Act may be cited as the Latent Damage Act 1986.

(2) In this Act—

'the 1980 Act' has the meaning given by section 1; and

"action" includes any proceeding in a court of law, an arbitration and any new claim within the meaning of section 35 of the 1980 Act (new claims in pending actions).

(3) This Act shall come into force at the end of the period of two months beginning with the date on which it is passed.

(4) This Act extends to England and Wales only.

Appendix 3

Foreign Limitation Periods Act 1984

An Act to provide for any law relating to the limitation of actions to be treated, for the purposes of cases in which effect is given to foreign law or to determinations by foreign courts, as a matter of substance rather than as a matter of procedure. [24th May 1984]

1 Application of foreign limitation law

(1) Subject to the following provisions of this Act, where in any action or proceedings in a court in England and Wales the law of any other country falls (in accordance with rules of private international law applicable by any such court) to be taken into account in the determination of any matter—

(*a*) the law of that other country relating to limitation shall apply in respect of that matter for the purposes of the action or proceedings; and

(*b*) except where that matter falls within subsection (2) below, the law of England and Wales relating to limitation shall not so apply.

(2) A matter falls within this subsection if it is a matter in the determination of which both the law of England and Wales and the law of some other country fall to be taken into account.

(3) The law of England and Wales shall determine for the purposes of any law applicable by virtue of subsection (1)(*a*) above whether, and the time at which, proceedings have been commenced in respect of any matter; and, accordingly, section 35 of the Limitation Act 1980 (new claims in pending proceedings) shall apply in relation to time limits applicable by virtue of subsection (1)(*a*) above as it applies in relation to time limits under that Act.

(4) A court in England and Wales, in exercising in pursuance of subsection (1)(*a*) above any discretion conferred by the law of any other country, shall so far as practicable exercise that discretion in the manner in which it is exercised in comparable cases by the courts of that other country.

(5) In this section "law", in relation to any country, shall not include rules of private international law applicable by the courts of that country or, in the case of England and Wales, this Act.

2 Exceptions to s 1

(1) In any case in which the application of section 1 above would to any extent conflict (whether under subsection (2) below or otherwise) with public policy, that section shall not apply to the extent that its application would so conflict.

(2) The application of section 1 above in relation to any action or proceedings shall conflict with public policy to the extent that its application would cause undue hardship to a person who is, or might be made, a party to the action or proceedings.

(3) Where, under a law applicable by virtue of section 1(1)(*a*) above for the purposes of any action or proceedings, a limitation period is or may be extended or interrupted in respect of the absence of a party to the action or proceedings from any specified jurisdiction or country, so much of that law as provides for the extension or interruption shall be disregarded for those purposes.

(4) In section 2(1) of the Limitation (Enemies and War Prisoners) Act 1945 (which in relation to cases involving enemy aliens and war prisoners extends certain limitation periods), in the definition of "statute of limitation", at the end, there shall be inserted the words—

"and, in a case to which section 1(1) of the Foreign Limitation Periods Act 1984 applies, so much of the law of any country outside England and Wales as applies by virtue of that Act.".

3 Foreign judgments on limitation points

Where a court in any country outside England and Wales has determined any matter wholly or partly by reference to the law of that or any other country (including England and Wales) relating to limitation, then, for the purposes of the law relating to the effect to be given in England and Wales to that determination, that court shall, to the extent that it has so determined the matter, be deemed to have determined it on its merits.

4 Meaning of law relating to limitation

(1) Subject to subsection (3) below, references in this Act to the law of any country (including England and Wales) relating to limitation shall, in relation to any matter, be construed as references to so much of the relevant law of that country as (in any manner) makes provision with respect to a limitation period applicable to the bringing of proceedings in respect of that matter in the courts of that country and shall include—

(*a*) references to so much of that law as relates to, and to the effect of, the application, extension, reduction or interruption of that period; and
(*b*) a reference, where under that law there is no limitation period which is so applicable, to the rule that such proceedings may be brought within an indefinite period.

(2) In subsection (1) above "relevant law", in relation to any country, means the procedural and substantive law applicable, apart from any rules of private international law, by the courts of that country.

(3) References in this Act to the law of England and Wales relating to limitation shall not include the rules by virtue of which a court may, in the exercise of any discretion, refuse equitable relief on the grounds of acquiescence or otherwise; but, in applying those rules to a case in relation to which the law of any country outside England and Wales is applicable by virtue of section 1(1)(*a*) above (not being a law that provides for a limitation period that has expired), a court in England and Wales shall have regard, in particular, to the provisions of the law that is so applicable.

5 Application of Act to arbitrations

The references to any other limitation enactment in section 34 of the Limitation Act 1980 (application of limitation enactments to arbitration) include references to sections 1, 2 and 4 of this Act; and, accordingly, in subsection (5) of the said section 34, the reference to the time prescribed by a limitation enactment has effect for the purposes of any case to which section 1 above applies as a reference to the limitation period (if any) applicable by virtue of section 1 above.

6 Application to Crown

(1) This Act applies in relation to any action or proceedings by or against the Crown as it applies in relation to actions and proceedings to which Crown is not a party.

(2) For the purposes of this section references to an action or proceedings by or against the Crown include references to—

(*a*) any action or proceedings by or against Her Majesty in right of the Duchy of Lancaster;
(*b*) any action or proceedings by or against any Government department or any officer of the Crown as such or any person acting on behalf of the Crown;
(*c*) any action or proceedings by or against the Duke of Cornwall.

7 Short title, commencement, transitional provision and extent

(1) This Act may be cited as the Foreign Limitation Periods Act 1984.

(2) This Act shall come into force on such day as the Lord Chancellor may by order made by statutory instrument appoint.

(3) Nothing in this Act shall—

(*a*) affect any action, proceedings or arbitration commenced in England and Wales before the day appointed under subsection (2) above; or
(*b*) apply in relation to any matter if the limitation period which, apart from this Act, would have been applied in respect of that matter in England and Wales expired before that day.

(4) This Act extends to England and Wales only.

Index

"Everyone directly or indirectly involved in the vastly expanding holiday industry, be they tour operators, travel agents, solicitors, barristers, arbitrators, consumer organisations or whatever, will be interested to read this unique and excellent little book produced by two solicitors with extensive practical experience in the field."

LAW SOCIETY'S GAZETTE

A Practical Guide to Package Holiday Law and Contracts brings together the various elements of the law as they apply to the travel industry and to package holidays in particular. It explains the structure of the industry and the special positions of both tour operator and travel agent, including the role of ABTA; and discusses the circumstances in which claims may be brought and likely damages arising from them.

Subjects featured include;

• Structure of the holiday industry • Legal duties of travel agents and tour operators • Circumstances which can lead to claims • Legal principles for assessing damage • Contracts with hoteliers and airlines • Insolvency of tour operators and travel agents • Roles of ABTA and CAA and the ATOL regulations

The book covers all the relevant statute and case law including a number of important but hitherto unreported cases.

The third edition has been fully revised and updated to include the regulations implementing the EC Directive on package travel, package holidays and package tours, which was effective from early 1993.

These regulations introduced wide-ranging criminal offences and civil liabilities for both tour operators and travel agents in respect of the marketing, sale and performance of package holidays. In addition they imposed compulsory requirements to provide financial security.

Priced at £29.95 only, this invaluable book is essential reading to all those involved in and advising on travel and tourism.

Satisfaction guaranteed or your money back

When you receive your order, if you are not entirely satisfied that it will be a major benefit to you in your work, simply return it in saleable condition within 21 days and we will refund your payment or cancel your invoice without question.

How to order

To order your copy of **A Practical Guide to Package Holiday Law and Contracts**, simply write to Tolley Publishing Company Ltd. Tolley House, 2 Addiscombe Road, Croydon CR9 5AF, or ring our telephone order line on 081-686-0115.

Tolley

ISBN 0 85459 810-3 336 Pages £29.95 May 1993

Notes

Notes